Amazing ME

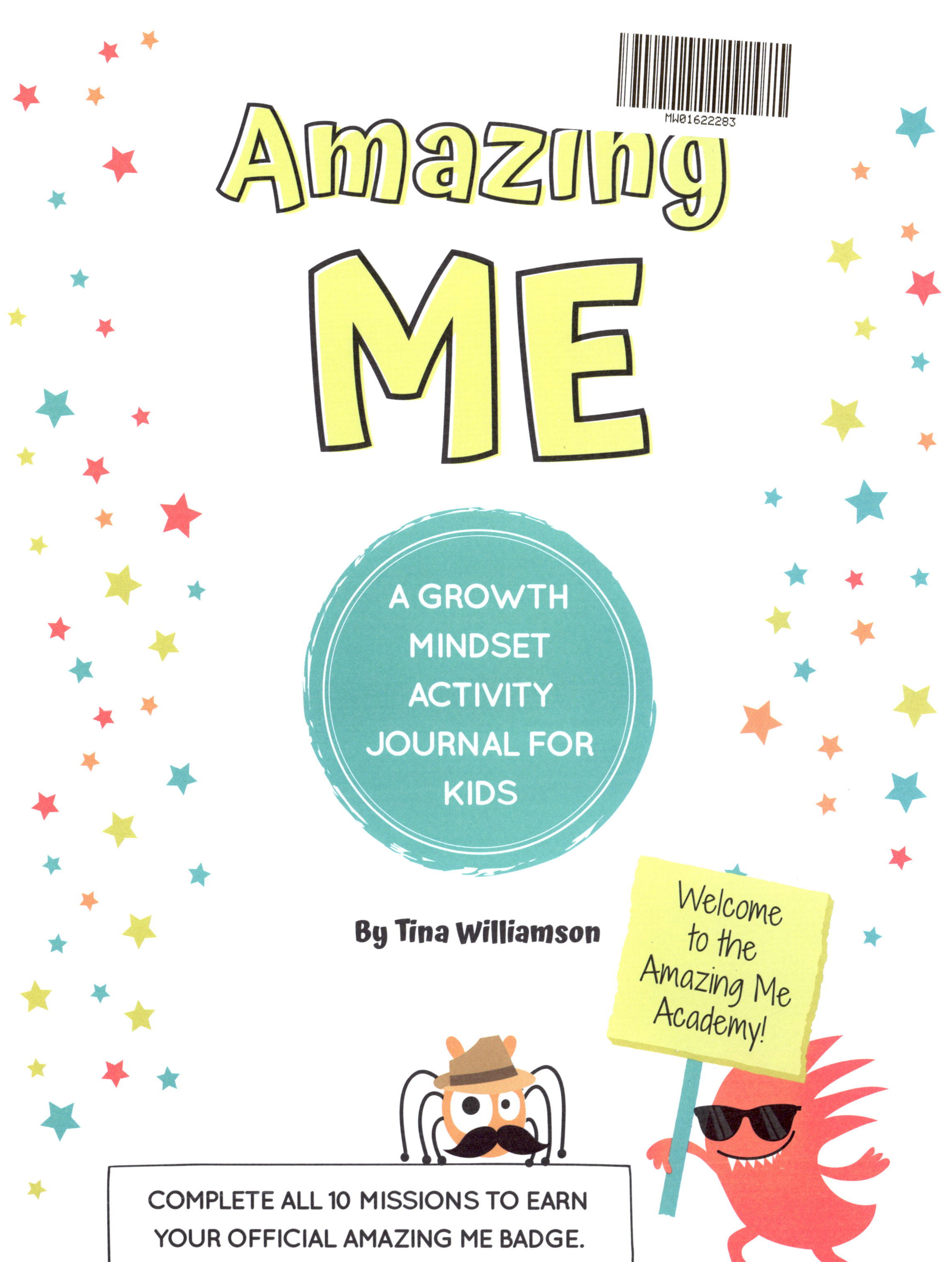

By Tina Williamson

COMPLETE ALL 10 MISSIONS TO EARN YOUR OFFICIAL AMAZING ME BADGE.

Published by
PESI Publishing
PESI, Inc.
3839 White Ave
Eau Claire, WI 54703

Cover: Jennifer Wilson-Gaetz
Editing: Jenessa Jackson
Layout: Tina Williamson and Jennifer Wilson-Gaetz

ISBN: 9781683734208

Printed in the United States of America

About the Author

Tina Williamson is a mom, a writer, and the founder of *Mindfulmazing*, a slice of the internet that is passionate about raising mindful, resilient, and compassionate kids. *Mindfulmazing* was initially created for her son, Liam, so that he could grow up in a supported, positive, and encouraging environment, but it's now grown to a community of thousands of parents, teachers, and practitioners from around the world who are also passionate about helping our youth feel confident and secure. Tina has a strong background in mindfulness and is committed to sharing calming strategies, positive parenting tips, and growth mindset resources. She's passionate about dispelling the myth that a misbehaving child is a "bad" child. There are no bad kids, only kids crying out for help. Tina was born and raised in Ontario, Canada, and when she's not writing or creating, she's usually lost in an adventure, trying to keep up with her wild-hearted son. She also loves patios, sunny days, live music, friends, and yoga (in no particular order). Find her on the web at www.mindfulmazing.com.

Dedication

For my son, Liam Livingstone,
my reason for everything.

Welcome to Amazing Me!

Amazing Me is an activity journal just for you! It has 10 special missions to help you learn new and exciting things about yourself.

These missions will help you discover how to be grateful, mindful, and kind. You'll also learn how to develop healthier habits, set goals, identify your strengths and weaknesses, and so much more!

Each mission is full of fun activities and special assignments for you to complete—and when you do, you'll get your official certificate for that mission. Collect all 10 certificates to become a special agent and earn your Amazing Me badge!

This training will equip you with a powerful growth mindset that will help you tackle anything that can and will come up in your life.

One more thing: This is a PG-13 symbol, and you will see this symbol sprinkled on a few pages throughout your missions. When you see this symbol, ask a grown-up for help reading through that page, just in case you don't understand something being discussed.

HELLO!

We are your mission partners from the Amazing Me Academy. We are here to pump you up and help you complete each mission. See you on the inside!

JOURNALING IS AMAZING!

HERE'S WHY...

WRITING DOWN **THOUGHTS** & **FEELINGS...**

- CALMS YOU DOWN!
- LETS YOU GET TO KNOW YOURSELF!
- MAKES YOU FEEL GOOD!
- HELPS YOU CONCENTRATE AND FOCUS!
- INSPIRES CREATIVITY!
- BOOSTS PROBLEM SOLVING!

____

(your name here)

IF YOU WISH TO DEDICATE YOUR JOURNAL TO SOMEONE SPECIAL, WRITE THEIR NAME HERE:

____

TOP-SECRET MISSIONS

- ❐ MISSION 1: Who Are You? 7
- ❐ MISSION 2: Catch a Big Dream. 19
- ❐ MISSION 3: Find the Missing Gratitude . . 33
- ❐ MISSION 4: Mindful Superpowers 47
- ❐ MISSION 5: Investigate Big Emotions 61
- ❐ MISSION 6: Chase Down Happiness 75
- ❐ MISSION 7: Explore Your Strengths. 91
- ❐ MISSION 8: Confidence Cadet 107
- ❐ MISSION 9: Goal Getter. 121
- ❐ MISSION 10: The Power of Kindness 139

MISSION 1

COMPLETE ALL THE ASSIGNMENTS IN MISSION "WHO ARE YOU?" TO RECEIVE YOUR FIRST SPECIAL AGENT CERTIFICATE!

ALL ABOUT ME!

MY NAME IS:

Class of:

My Favorite Color:

My Pets:

I Love:

When I Grow Up

I want to be:

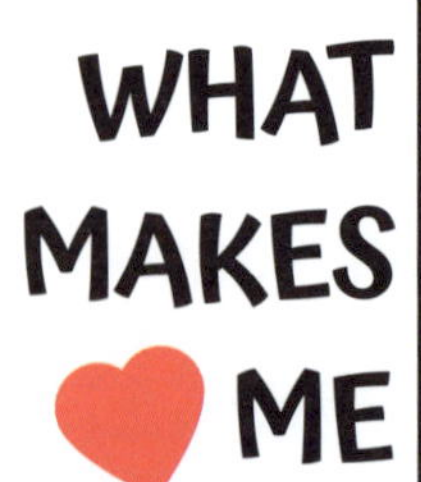

My Favorite Animal:

My Favorite Food:

My Best Friend:

My School:

My Teacher:

All families are different. Your friends' families might look completely different from your family. And you know what? That's okay! That's great! What makes a family a family is having people who love and care for one another.

Draw a picture of your family here:

Maybe your family has one mommy and one daddy. Or maybe your family has no mommy or daddy. Or maybe your family has no mommy or daddy but a rockin' grandma. You might even have two mommies or two daddies. Your family might be made up of aunts, friends, cousins, or even annoying siblings. Any mix is fine. **It's always love that makes a family a family.**

MY SUPERPOWERS

List your superpowers in the thought bubbles.

IDEAS

My brain is powerful.
I'm creative.
I'm kind.
I tell funny jokes.
I'm a good friend.

I try hard.
I don't give up.
I love helping people.
I'm great at sports.
I rock at school.

I'm brave.
I have super strength.
I love trying new things.
I keep a positive mindset.
I eat brussels sprouts.

TIME CAPSULE

A time capsule is a collection of present-day items that you hide away for your future self to look back on—and this journal could be yours! One day you'll flip through these pages and remember who you were, what you liked, and what was going on in the world at that time.

In the space below, write, tape, or draw things that are important in your life right now.

IDEAS OF THINGS TO INCLUDE:

- ❒ Special photos
- ❒ A letter to your future self
- ❒ Artwork
- ❒ A story you've written
- ❒ A recipe for your favorite food
- ❒ The words to your favorite song

MY HANDPRINT

TRACE YOUR HAND BELOW. THEN COLOR IT IN!

WHAT MAKES YOU SPECIAL?

Everyone is unique and special, like a rainbow. Start to pay attention to what makes you, *you*! Let's call this *noticing the colors of your rainbow*. Everyone's rainbow looks different. Below, fill in the things that make you special.

One special skill I have is:

I always try to:

Most of the time, I feel:

My friends would describe me as:

Something I always want to remember:

What I love most about me:

The colors of my RAINBOW

MISSION REPORT

What 5 words do you think best describe YOU?

1.

2.

3.

4.

5.

If you could have 1 wish, what would it be?

If you weren't afraid of anything, what would you do?

"THE THINGS THAT MAKE ME DIFFERENT ARE THE THINGS THAT MAKE ME, ME."

Piglet from *Winnie the Pooh*

Certificate of Completion

This certificate is presented to special agent:

for completing the top-secret training mission:

WHO ARE YOU?

Presented by: The Amazing Me Academy

MISSION 2

CATCH A BIG DREAM

COMPLETE ALL THE ASSIGNMENTS IN MISSION "CATCH A BIG DREAM" TO RECEIVE YOUR NEXT SPECIAL AGENT CERTIFICATE!

THE WORLD IS YOUR OYSTER

THIS MISSION IS ALL ABOUT DREAMING BIG!

Dreams are important, no matter how big or small. Your dream might be to walk on the moon, to invent a new ice cream flavor, or to become a doctor, a construction worker, or even a famous sports player. Your dream might be to learn how to ride a bike or to play your favorite song on the piano. It's up to you!

Having dreams pushes you to try new things, get stronger, and learn more. Anything is possible—and it all starts with one small step!

★ Dreaming big is exciting!

★ The impossible happens all the time!

★ Setting goals will help you achieve them!

★ You can do hard things!

★ Today is your day!

"Whether you think you can, or you think you can't— you're right."

Henry Ford

MISSION NOTES

What are your dreams?

What is standing in your way?

If you won a million dollars...
what would you do?

"Shoot for the moon. Even if you miss, you'll land among the stars."

Norman Vincent Peale

"IT ONLY TAKES ONE PERSON WITH A BIG DREAM TO MAKE A BIG DIFFERENCE."

ALBERT EINSTEIN

PG-13

Albert Einstein was one super smart man. He is one of the most famous scientists and inventors **the world has ever seen!**

He developed a very important scientific theory, which led to the invention of all kinds of things we use every day, like:

- TVs
- Garage door openers
- Satellites
- GPS systems

But did you know? When Einstein was young, various teachers told him that he wouldn't amount to anything. But boy, were they wrong!

Despite others doubting him, Einstein followed his dreams and accomplished BIG things.

FUN FACTS:

Einstein was obsessed with magnets!

He loved science and math. By the time he was 16, he had published his first scientific paper.

Einstein was very disorganized. He always had uncombed hair and never wore socks!

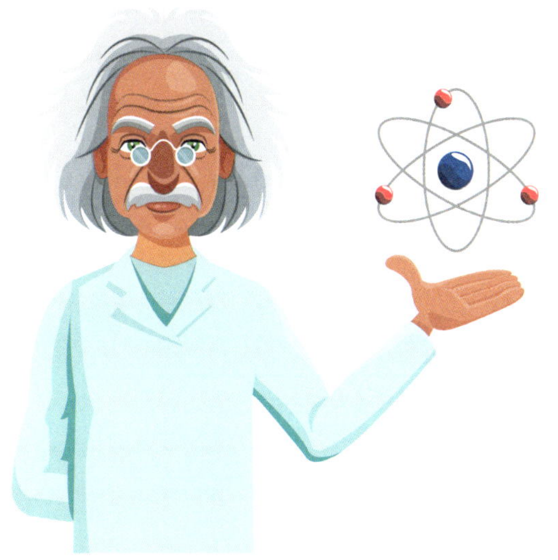

One of Einstein's favorite things to do was to sit by a lake and write down his thoughts. Einstein loved to use his imagination, and he famously said:

"Imagination is more important than knowledge."

Einstein is a story of great success—one that you can take spoonfuls of inspiration from.

Do you have an idea of something you'd like to invent? Write it here!

____

____

What steps do you need to take to get there?

____

____

____

____

____

____

____

____

____

____

____

DRAW YOUR INVENTION

START DREAMING

PG-13

Are you wondering how to dream big? Consider these 5 things:

1. BE BORED!

Did you know being bored is good for you? It's true! It's where creativity is born! Try it. Allow yourself to daydream or "do nothing" rather than automatically jumping on your phone or tablet or turning on the TV.

2. SHARE

Don't be afraid to share all your big ideas with those who love you. Sharing ideas gives you an army of support and encouragement.

3. EXPLORE

Take every chance you can to read, learn, grow, and try new things and ideas. Silence that voice in your head that says "I can't" when you try something hard.

4. BE OKAY WITH MISTAKES

Mistakes happen all the time, to everyone. The important thing is to keep trying to reach your dreams. Learn from mistakes and improve!

5. SET A GOAL

When you set a goal (like practicing tae kwon do daily), it can help you achieve your dreams (like achieving your black belt).

It can be a serious goal, like upping your reading level, or a super fun goal, like going camping. Once you know exactly what it is you want, you can focus your attention on taking the steps you need to achieve that goal.

Think big, dream big, and believe big—and the results will be BIG.

WHO SUPPORTS YOU?

Most of us have someone who knows us really well, whom we enjoy spending time with. Friends and family are special gifts in our lives.

Supportive relationships will help you get back up when you are feeling down.

Take a moment to think about the people who support you, such as friends, family members, teachers, coaches, or neighbors.

CREATE A VISION BOARD

A vision board is a collage of pictures and words that represent your biggest dreams. When you create a space that displays what you want in life, it can help bring those dreams to life.

INSTRUCTIONS

- Find a piece of poster board, construction paper, or cardboard to serve as your board.
- Gather other supplies you'll need:
  - Magazines
  - Tape
  - Photos
  - Markers
  - Stickers
  - Ribbons
  - Scissors
  - Glue
  - Old greeting cards
- Find some quiet time.
- Get creative! Fill your board up with anything that makes you feel happy or anything you'd like to see happen in your future. Basically, flip through magazines, greeting cards, and photos, and select images that are meaningful to you.

QUESTIONS

Ask yourself these questions to get inspiration for your board:

- What does your dream vacation look like?
- What is your favorite food?
- What do you want to be when you grow up?
- If you could design your own dream house or car, what would it look like?
- What are your favorite hobbies?
- What do you love about life right now?
- What are your biggest goals?
- Is there anyone you'd love to meet in person?
- How can you make a difference in the world?
- What do you look for in a friend?
- What kind of sports do you like?
- If you could have any superpower, what would it be?

"When you have a dream, you've got to grab it and never let it go."

Carol Burnett

MY BUCKET LIST

This is a list of things you REALLY want to do in the next few months!

MISSION REPORT

Name someone you think has accomplished something special:

What did they accomplish?

Ask a grown-up to tell you about someone they admire.
Write their answer below:

REACH FOR THE STARS

Certificate of Completion

This certificate is presented to special agent:

for completing the top-secret training mission:

CATCH A BIG DREAM

Presented by: The Amazing Me Academy

MISSION 3

FIND THE MISSING GRATITUDE

For those who want to see, feel,
and love all the good in life

COMPLETE ALL THE ASSIGNMENTS IN MISSION "FIND THE MISSING GRATITUDE" TO RECEIVE YOUR NEXT SPECIAL AGENT CERTIFICATE!

WHAT IS GRATITUDE?

GRATITUDE IS YOUR SECRET WEAPON

Gratitude involves focusing on the good things in our lives and being thankful for the things we have, the people we love, and the things we get to experience.

Sometimes we're so busy thinking about what we DON'T have that we forget about what we DO have. That's why this mission is about finding the missing gratitude. There is always something to be thankful for!

AND HERE'S WHY THIS MISSION IS SO IMPORTANT...

Gratitude doesn't just feel good—it's also good FOR you. Brain research tells us that your body and brain love positive thoughts!

One positive emotion leads to another. Gratitude moves your attention away from annoying negative thoughts and to fantastic happy thoughts.

Gratitude improves relationships. When you appreciate other people and what they do for you, it strengthens your relationships. And I'm not just talking about your family—you can feel grateful for your friends, your school, your community, and even yourself!

Gratitude leads to positive action. When you feel grateful for someone's kindness toward you, you are more likely to do something kind in return.

I bet there are SO many things you would miss from your life if they were suddenly gone. Take a moment and think about some of these things now.

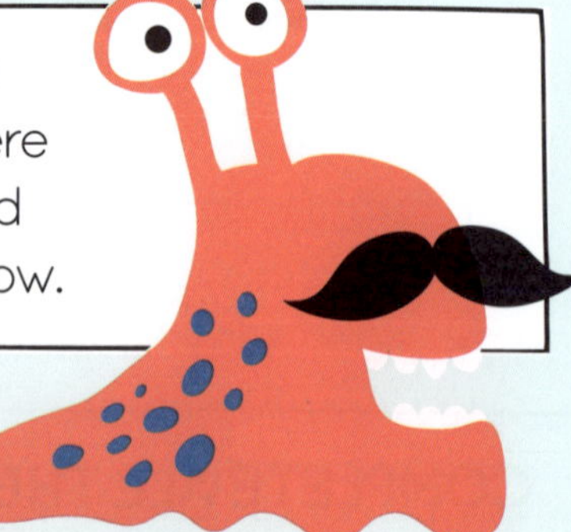

MISSION NOTES

3 things that happened in the last 24 hours that you're thankful for:

1.

2.

3.

What part did you have in making these 3 things happen?

Things and people you are grateful to have in your life:

MINI GRATITUDE ACTIVITIES

GRATITUDE SCAVENGER HUNT

Take it outside.

Who doesn't love a scavenger hunt? Beforehand, make a list of things to find. Then you can check them off as you go.

IDEAS:

- Something you love
- Something beautiful
- Something that's your favorite color
- Something in nature
- A neat sound
- A word
- Something that makes you happy

YOUR FAVORITE THINGS

This is a fun, easy game to play in the car. Simply take turns telling each other what you like about each of the items listed here (or you can add your own categories!).

PROMPT:

"My favorite thing about ___________ is..."

School • The Grown-Ups in My Life
Weekends • Summer • Holidays
Bedtime • Dinner

GRATITUDE DRAWINGS

Draw 1 of these 3 things:

★ Something that makes you happy ★ Someone who helps you ★ Something you think is fun

MAKE A GRATITUDE JAR

INGREDIENTS

- Jar or box
- Ribbon or stickers
- Paper
- Gratitude

INSTRUCTIONS

Cut 20 or so strips of paper. Write one thing you are thankful for on each strip of paper and put them in the jar. Then use ribbon or stickers to decorate the jar.

REMEMBER

It's often small moments that make life wonderful: a beautiful sunrise, fresh strawberries for lunch, a smile from a friend, or an encouraging hug from someone who loves you.

Taking the time to appreciate these moments helps you to LOVE your life and yourself.

GRATITUDE TAKES PRACTICE

Gratitude doesn't just happen! It's like learning how to do math: You need to practice.

Whenever you have a down day (and we all have them), you can pull a slip of paper from your gratitude jar and remind yourself of all the beautiful things in your life.

Have you ever heard the saying "Is your glass half full or half empty?" Well, gratitude is what makes your glass full. Life is beautiful, and gratitude reminds you that you have lots to be thankful for if you look for it.

THINGS I LOVE...

I love this color:

I love when my parent or guardian does this:

I love when my belly is full of:

I love when the weather is:

I love to do this when I'm not in school:

I love this about animals:

I love when my friends do this:

I love this about school:

I love my bedroom because:

THINGS TO BE GRATEFUL FOR

Art, music, bees, trees, stars, castles, butterflies, fish, flowers, clean water, yummy food, kind teachers, school, new school supplies, pumpkin patches, hot chocolate, campfires, beaches, wizards, puddles, fall leaf piles, candy, photographs, sunsets, memories, clean air, the sun, friends and family, surprises, presents

Now you name 3 things!

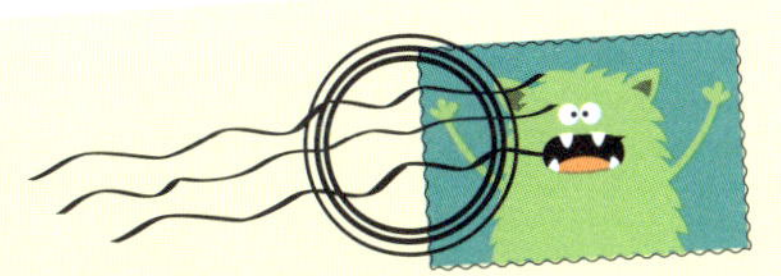

Hey cadet,

Is there someone in your life you'd like to thank? Perhaps someone who has done something nice for you lately? It can be anyone: a teacher, parent/guardian, friend, or neighbor. Write a message and thank them. Tell them what they did that was nice and how it made you feel. Cut out your letter and give it to your special someone. Now take a moment and imagine **how good this person will feel** reading your special thank-you letter!

WRITE A THANK-YOU LETTER

Dear ______________________,

I'm grateful to be

ME! Here's why:

☆ ______________________

____

☆ ______________________

____

☆ ______________________

____

☆ ______________________

____

☆ ______________________

____

ATTITUDE IS EVERYTHING!

On the clipboard, write down at least 5 positive things about YOU! Whether or not you believe it yet, you have so many amazing qualities.

HERE ARE SOME IDEAS:

What are you good at in school?

Have you helped anyone lately?

What are your 3 best qualities?

Are you proud of a recent accomplishment?

Are you trying harder to learn something?

What sports are you good at?

Do you love music? Art? Dance? Martial arts? Books? Coloring?

MISSION REPORT

GRATITUDE JOURNAL

Things you are thankful for today:

1.

2.

3.

Pick a positive word—like **fun, calm, generous,** or **beautiful**—and name one way that word showed up in your day today. In other words, write something awesome that happened TODAY in this space.

Circle how you feel right now:

sad

confused

neutral

upset

happy

playful

What was the most challenging part of your day?

"COUNT YOUR RAINBOWS, NOT YOUR THUNDERSTORMS."

Alyssa Knight, Age 12

Certificate of Completion

This certificate is presented to special agent:

for completing the top-secret training mission:

FIND THE MISSING GRATITUDE

Presented by: The Amazing Me Academy

MISSION 4

MINDFUL SUPERPOWERS

COMPLETE ALL THE ASSIGNMENTS IN MISSION "MINDFUL SUPERPOWERS" TO RECEIVE YOUR NEXT SPECIAL AGENT CERTIFICATE!

WHAT IS MINDFULNESS?

Mindfulness simply means noticing what is happening right now, like what you see and smell, or how you feel, or what your mind is thinking and how you are reacting.

Noticing helps you:

With school, sports, and hobbies

Paying attention has BIG benefits. When you pay attention, you're improving your concentration, and this helps your brain grow stronger. You can ALWAYS achieve more with better focus.

Calm down when you are upset

Your mind is sneaky, and when you pay attention to what it's up to, you can make better decisions. We all deal with BIG feelings, and when you start to notice these emotions, you can stop them from overpowering you.

Develop stronger relationships

Have you ever been so focused on what you wanted to say that you didn't listen to what others were saying? Taking the time to listen helps others feel cared for, which is a great way to connect.

Sleep better

Yep, learning how to relax and calm your mind will help you settle down and stop your mind from racing when you hit the pillow.

See how exciting the world is

When you tune in to what's around you, it opens up possibilities and helps you see the world with fresh eyes.

AND HERE'S THE BEST PART:

Mindfulness is free, and you can do it anytime, anywhere. In this mission you will learn all about mighty mindfulness!

Tuning In with YOUR 5 SENSES

This simple exercise can help you calm down in a mindful way by using your 5 senses to tune in to the things around you.

When you mindfully focus on whatever is happening *right now*, you'll notice things you normally wouldn't pay attention to. This is called "savoring," and it helps you see the world with fresh eyes. This makes each moment seem new. It's an adventure in noticing—and the more you notice, the more you see!

"Be happy in the moment, that's enough. Each moment is all we need, not more."

Mother Teresa

HOW TO BE MINDFUL

1. NOTICE WHAT'S HAPPENING AROUND AND INSIDE YOU

Become aware of the way your body feels. Notice the tingling in your fingers, the butterflies in your stomach, or the way the floor feels under your feet. Also start to notice how you are reacting to those feelings. Don't beat yourself up about anything. Just notice.

2. DO ONE THING AT A TIME

When you're doing something, whether it's playing with your toys, doing a school assignment, or taking a shower, just do that one thing. If you're doing homework, just do homework, don't check your phone or watch TV at the same time. If you're eating dinner, just eat dinner, don't play with toys or pester your brother. This improves your ability to concentrate, and when we grow our concentration skills, we can accomplish great things.

3. ACCEPT THE THINGS YOU CAN'T CONTROL

You have no control over many things in life (like weather and other people). Be open to what's happening in the moment, even if you don't like it. Try to find the good in every situation. You can find something positive, if you look.

4. GO EASY ON YOURSELF

Remember that everything comes in time, and much like cooking an egg, if you try to rush it, the yolk will break and make a big mess. Be patient with yourself and others.

DON'T FORGET TO TAKE DEEP BREATHS, SMILE, AND GET OUTSIDE FOR LOTS OF FRESH AIR!

JUST BREATHE.

"The little things? The little moments? They aren't little."

Jon Kabat-Zinn

STARFISH FINGERS

Start Here

EACH EVENING BEFORE BED, TRACE THE FINGERS OF YOUR HAND, OR TAKE TURNS TRACING YOUR GROWN-UPS' OR SIBLINGS' HANDS.

INSTRUCTIONS

Sit, lay, or stand comfortably with your back straight. Open the palm of one hand wide. Now, using the pointer finger of your opposite hand, trace your fingers while breathing. Breathe in as you trace up one side of your thumb—1, 2, 3, 4—and breathe out as you trace down the other side of your thumb—1, 2, 3, 4. Repeat for all 5 fingers.

FEEL YOUR BODY RELAX!

BRILLIANT BREATHING

Learning to pay attention to your breath helps calm your body and lets you relax! Here's how to take a proper full breath...

 Get in a comfy position. You can be standing, sitting, or lying down on the floor.

 Place your hands on your belly, and slowly breathe in through your nose. Consider closing your eyes. Otherwise, let your eyelids get heavy in a "soft gaze."

 Breathe all the way to the bottom of your belly. Hold your breath for a count of 2.

 Next, let all the air out through your mouth. Feel your shoulders relax as you exhale.

 Repeat this as many times as you need.

Set an alarm every couple of hours reminding you to take a few deep belly breaths.

STOP! AND JUST BREATHE

Practice taking full breaths by tracing the octagon below with your finger as you breathe in and out.

BREATHING EXERCISES

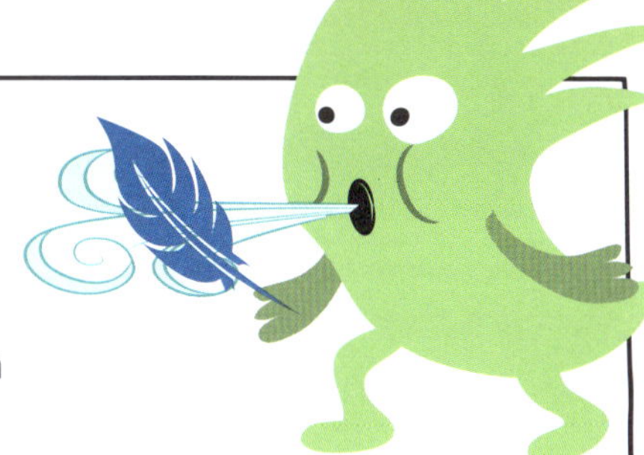

FEATHER BREATHING

Collect a feather or pretend to hold one. Take a deep breath, inhale for a count of 3, then slowly exhale through your nose. As you exhale, gently blow your breath up one side of the feather and down the other.

TIMER BREATHING

Set a timer for 1 minute. Sit cross-legged on the floor, in a chair, or outside in the grass, and breathe in and out deeply (without talking) until the timer goes off. Pay close attention to any sounds you hear around you or things you feel in your body. Just notice. If your mind wanders off to thoughts of other things, pull your thoughts back to only noticing sounds around you and feelings inside you.

ONE NOSTRIL BREATH

This exercise is silly and fun. Place your finger over one nostril, then breathe in deeply. Next, switch your finger to the other nostril as you breathe out. Once you have exhaled slowly, switch and repeat. Practice this exercise for no more than 2 minutes.

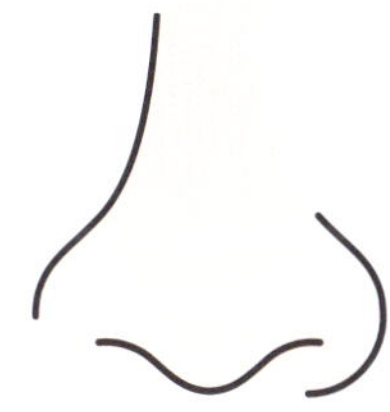

BUMBLE BEE BREATH

Sitting comfortably with your legs crossed, breathe in through your nose for a count of 4. As you breathe out, make a buzzing or humming sound, like you're a bee. Variation: When you exhale, place your fingers in your ears and hum out as you exhale.

BALLOON BREATHING

Pretend that your belly is a balloon. Take a slow, deep breath in and notice how your belly gets bigger, like a balloon. Next, breathe out and notice how your belly deflates, also like a balloon. Do 5 rounds of this rhythmic breathing.

VISUALIZATIONS

Picture a peaceful scene. It can be a waterfall in a forest, rolling waves at the beach, or a green meadow full of flowers. Now picture yourself in this peaceful scene. What's it like? What do you feel, see, hear, smell, and even taste while you're in this place? Write about it below.

Describe your scene in crystal-clear detail:

Draw your scene:

FOCUS FLOWER

This fun mindfulness exercise helps you see things better. Find a flower or plant to use as your "focus living object." You will look at this living object very closely and notice all its intricate and delicate details.

Once you have your flower or plant, sit on the floor with your legs crossed or on a chair if that's more comfortable. Sit up tall and reach the top of your head toward the sky, but keep your neck and shoulders relaxed. Now close your eyes and take 5 deep breaths.

Open your eyes and examine your object. Notice the colors, smell, intricate lines, and details. Notice the texture and shape. Notice the petals (or leaves) and stem. Does your flower or plant look different when you pay attention? Can you see how miraculous and incredible it is? There are so many details you've likely never noticed before.

"If we could see the miracle of a single flower clearly, our whole life would change."

BUDDHA

Describe your flower or plant below.

What color is it? What size? What shape? What does it smell like?

____

____

____

____

Discuss what you see differently in your flower or plant after examining it closely:

____

____

____

____

MISSION REPORT

MINDFULNESS JOURNAL

Set a timer and sit quietly for 2 minutes. Practice the deep breathing exercises from the previous pages, and simply notice what's happening in your body and mind. Then fill out this page.

How did you feel before sitting quietly?

What feelings came up in your body and mind during these 2 minutes of quiet time? Did your mind wander? What did you think about?

What was it like to sit still for 2 minutes?

- ❒ I didn't like it
- ❒ It was hard
- ❒ It was easier than I thought
- ❒ I felt peaceful and calm

Circle how you feel right now:

sad

confused

neutral

upset

happy

playful

"MINDS ARE LIKE PARACHUTES—THEY ONLY FUNCTION WHEN OPEN."

THOMAS DEWAR

Certificate of Completion

This certificate is presented to special agent:

for completing the top-secret training mission:

MINDFUL SUPERPOWERS

Presented by: The Amazing Me Academy

MISSION 5

INVESTIGATE BIG EMOTIONS

COMPLETE ALL THE ASSIGNMENTS IN MISSION "INVESTIGATE BIG EMOTIONS" TO RECEIVE YOUR NEXT SPECIAL AGENT CERTIFICATE!

PG-13

MEET THE EMOTIONS

ANGER

Anger is a powerful feeling that arises when things aren't going your way. When you're angry, you might feel it in your body. You might clench your fists, or your face might get red and hot. When you are in this mood, you might feel scared, frustrated, jealous, confused, anxious, or annoyed.

HAPPINESS

Happiness is when you feel pleasure, joy, and satisfaction. When you feel happy, you often feel energized and positive. You might describe this mood as silly, joyful, brave, excited, or optimistic.

SADNESS

Sadness is what you feel when you lose something important, feel helpless, or feel disappointed. When you feel sad, you might have low energy levels, become quiet, or want to be left alone. You might describe this mood in several ways, including tired, bored, lonely, worried, overwhelmed, or disappointed.

CALMNESS

When you feel calm, you often feel relaxed and peaceful. You aren't bothered or upset. You might describe this mood in any number of ways, including kind, loving, grateful, or reflective.

How many of these emotions have you felt?

"Feelings are just visitors. Let them come and go."

Mooji

MISSION NOTES

Describe the last time you felt so angry you wanted to scream:

Describe the last time you felt scared:

Circle how you feel right now:

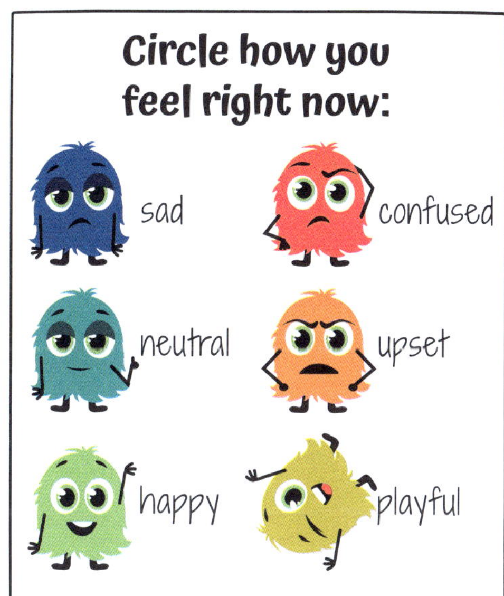

Describe the last time you cried:

Describe the last time you felt worried:

WHY DO I FEEL SO MUCH?

PG-13

We all feel a wide range of emotions. This is completely normal.

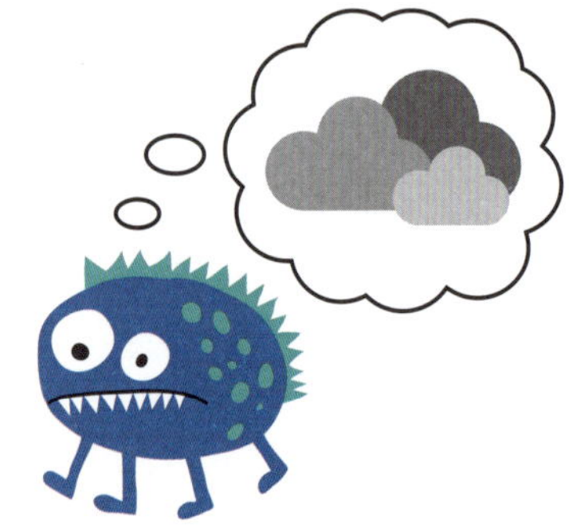

Everyone feels happiness, loneliness, jealousy, anxiety, anger, joy, fear, and more! There are over 25 different human emotions, and **all of them are normal, even the ones that don't feel great.** Allow yourself to feel whatever it is you are feeling. Don't be afraid to talk to a trusted friend or grown-up if your emotions feel too big or overwhelming.

To help you understand your emotions, take a moment to think about the weather. Like the weather, your emotions come and go, and no matter how strong they are, they will pass.

We can't control the weather or change it. It might not be what we want, but we CAN get through it, and it will eventually pass. We can accept the stormy days the same way we welcome the sunny ones.

This is a super-simple exercise where you use the weather to describe your feelings. For example:

- If you're happy, you might feel like a sunny day.
- If you're sad, you might feel like a rainy day.
- If you're excited, you might feel like a tornado.
- If you're lonely, you might feel like a snowy day.

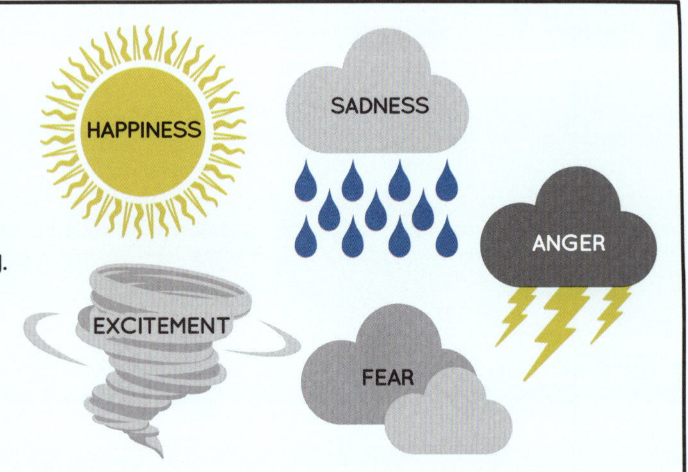

Try new ways to describe your emotions using the weather!

Pay attention to how you feel. Do you feel happy, sad, bored, tired, jealous, anxious, calm, or something else?

Can you describe what you are feeling using only the weather?

Be a super detective like "Nate the Great."

DETECTIVE ______________________

SPECIAL CASE ASSIGNMENT:

INVESTIGATE BIG EMOTIONS

Have you ever used a magnifying glass? Well, a magnifying glass makes things look larger and helps you see things you've never seen before, like really tiny insects. It lets you discover a whole new world! **Today you will use your magnifying glass to look inside you!** Investigate situations that made you feel the emotions listed in each of the boxes below. Jot down what made you feel that way and why.

CALM	HAPPY	EXCITED
BORED	ANGRY	PROUD
SAD	LOVED	SURPRISED

HOW TO HANDLE BIG EMOTIONS

You are the boss of your brain! That means you can learn cool new tricks to use when powerful feelings take over. Remember, it's normal to feel a lot of different emotions, and all emotions are important! Use these steps next time a big emotion comes on.

1 When in doubt, just breathe

Use the breathing exercises from the "Mindful Superpowers" mission, or simply breathe in for 3 seconds and out for 4 seconds. Repeat 10 times.

2 Step back

When big feelings take over, can you step back as if you are watching a movie? If someone in the movie was feeling the way you are, what would you say to them? What would you think?

3 Use a calming strategy

The next time you feel upset, try these strategies to calm down your body and mind.

Use only kind words	Drink a glass of water	Water the plants	Count to 10	Make a fist
Listen	Think before you say your next sentence	Trace the fingers on your hand twice	Freeze for 5 seconds	Go outside and look up at the sky
Hug someone or hug a tree!	Breathe deeply	Take a break	Ask for help or talk to a friend	Play with a fidget toy
Say a silly word	Do 10 jumping jacks	Write down your feelings	Read or journal	Put your hands in your pockets

Create your own calm-down plan....

  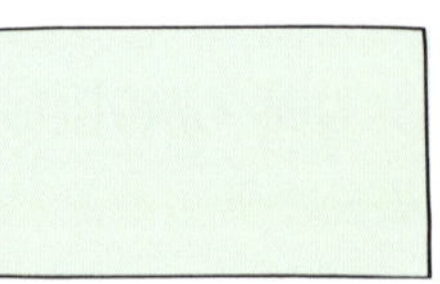 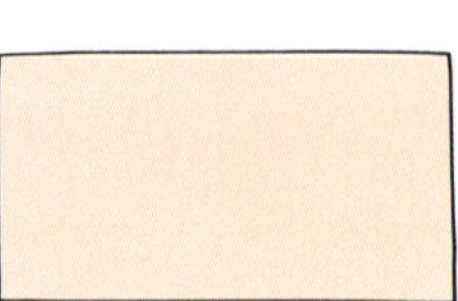 

4 Figure out what pushes your buttons

It's helpful to know what makes you upset so you can have your calm-down plan ready to go when you find yourself in one of these situations!

Place a check mark next to the situations that push your buttons:

- Being in a noisy place
- Needing to sit still
- Worrying something bad might happen
- Waiting
- Having too much homework
- Others not listening to you
- Being told no
- Feeling scared
- Being teased
- Loud noises
- Being touched
- Not being in control
- When others disagree with you
- Being in a crowded place
- Being interrupted
- Feeling left out
- Not understanding something
- Being criticized
- Needing to ask for help
- Being alone

What pushes your buttons?

We can't control everything that happens, but we can control how we react to what's happening. We CAN control what we think about things (our attitude) and how we respond to others when we feel big emotions.

Play this fun game with your siblings or grown-ups...

BEAR HUG TIME

Whenever you feel yourself getting ramped up, or if you notice someone in your family getting agitated, shout this phrase:

"Bear hug time!"

Everyone must stop what they are doing and hug as tightly as they can for 20 seconds.

Did you know? Hugs make you happier!

3 COOL FACTS ABOUT EMOTIONS

1. Emotions are contagious.
2. Forcing a smile releases a chemical in your brain that can make you happy.
3. The way you feel is always written on your face.

"Feelings are much like waves. We can't stop them from coming, but we can choose which one to surf."

Jonatan Mårtensson

Do you control your emotions or do they control you?

You are in control of your behavior (no matter how you feel!). Even when you're upset, you can still decide whether to make good choices or not-so-good choices.

Good Choices

Not-So-Good Choices

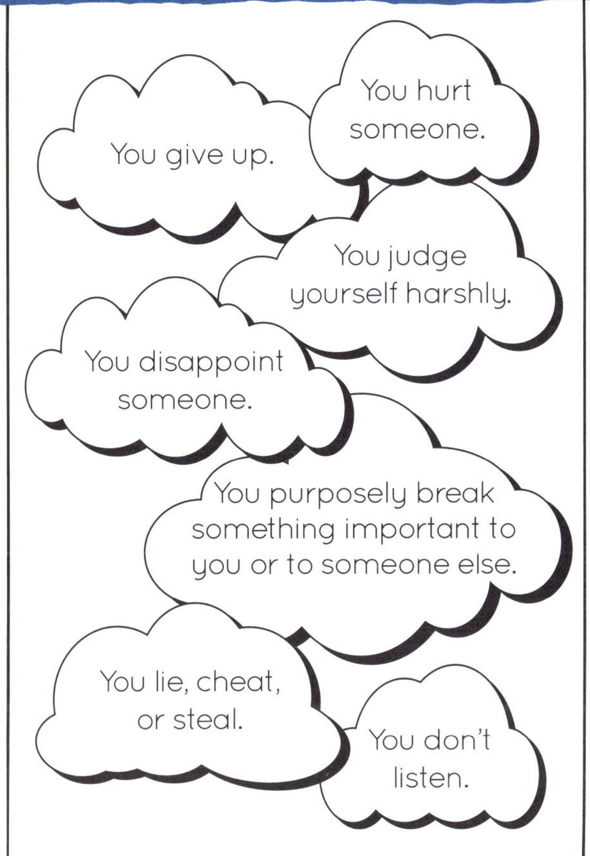

When you make good choices and are in control...

 You feel calmer.

 You grow stronger and smarter.

 You make friends easier.

 You do better in school.

 You feel better about yourself.

 You don't get in as much trouble.

Can you name another good thing about being in control?

MISSION REPORT

FEELINGS JOURNAL

DATE: / /

Today I am feeling:

Because:

But here's how I want to feel:

True or False (circle one)

I am in control of how I feel and how I react to those feelings.

True or False (circle one)

Feelings come and go, just like the weather.

One thing I can do to improve my mood when I'm feeling down:

"WHEN WE CAN TALK ABOUT OUR FEELINGS, THEY BECOME LESS OVERWHELMING, LESS UPSETTING, AND LESS SCARY."

Fred Rogers

Certificate of Completion

This certificate is presented to special agent:

for completing the top-secret training mission:

INVESTIGATE BIG EMOTIONS

Presented by: The Amazing Me Academy

MISSION 6

CHASE DOWN HAPPINESS

COMPLETE ALL THE ASSIGNMENTS IN MISSION "CHASE DOWN HAPPINESS" TO RECEIVE YOUR NEXT SPECIAL AGENT CERTIFICATE!

THE PURSUIT OF HAPPINESS

This mission is all about learning what makes you happy!

Here's the cool thing about happiness: YOU are in the driver's seat of your happiness. (I know you can't drive yet, but when we talk about happiness, YOU ARE THE DRIVER.) The weather doesn't control your happiness, and happiness isn't about how much money you have, or even if you have the coolest new toy. What makes you happy is what you think. If you think a new superhero toy is boring, then it will be. But if you think it's fantastic, then you'll certainly feel happy playing with it.

When we focus on positive thoughts, we feel good. And feeling good is what happiness is all about.

Do any of these feel-good activities make you happy?

- Playing with friends on nice, sunny days
- Going to a park or amusement park
- Having a big family dinner with cake for dessert

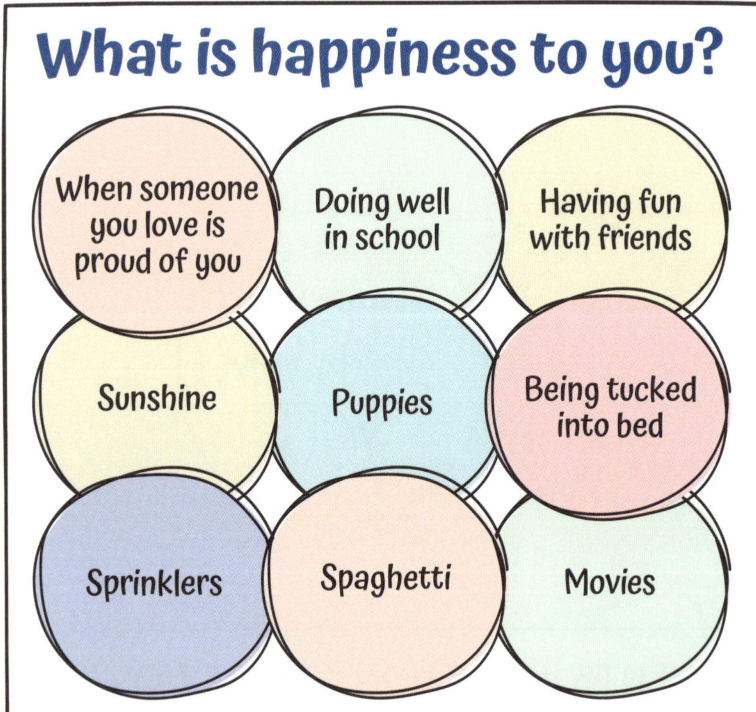

MISSION NOTES

What does happiness mean to you?

What makes you unhappy?

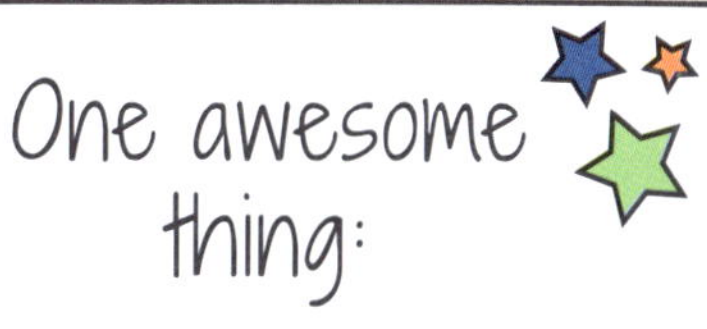

One awesome thing:

Draw a picture of something that brings a smile to your face:

HAPPY HABITS

A habit is something we do regularly without much thought. There are good habits (like saying nice things to others, brushing our teeth daily, and going to bed on time) and bad habits (like insulting others, biting our nails, eating too much sugar, and never brushing our teeth). When you develop good habits as a kid, it will help you be happy for your entire life!

DID YOU KNOW?

Exercise is an example of a good habit. Getting 20 minutes of exercise each day makes you happy!

When you exercise, special feel-good chemicals are released in your brain that can last over 12 hours—that's half a day! And what's equally neat is that exercise helps you sleep (and who doesn't need a few extra zzzs). Moving your body will also help you feel calm, focused, and strong.

FUN FACTS:

 Exercise helps you be social.

 Exercise improves your grades!

 Exercise makes your heart happy, and it just feels good!

Whether you are dancing, walking the dog, playing tag, or simply reaching down to touch your toes, ALL exercise benefits you.

YOU ARE WHAT YOU EAT

Eating healthy is another good habit! Eating whole foods like fruits, vegetables, and lean proteins will help you sharpen your mind, control your mood, and grow big and strong. It's also helpful to avoid too many sugary treats. For this assignment, see if you can:

 **Swap out an unhealthy snack for a healthy one**

 **Eat 2 fruits or veggies you love each day**

 **Help your parent or guardian prepare a meal**

If you have any food allergies, talk to your grown-ups.

HEALTHY HABITS TRACKER

Place a check mark beside the exercises you love:

- ❒ Basketball
- ❒ Soccer
- ❒ Hockey
- ❒ Baseball
- ❒ Playing tag
- ❒ Skipping
- ❒ Karate
- ❒ Tae kwon do
- ❒ Badminton
- ❒ Tennis
- ❒ Yoga
- ❒ Stretching
- ❒ Riding my bike
- ❒ Walking up and down the stairs
- ❒ Running through a sprinkler
- ❒ Playing at a splash pad
- ❒ Swimming
- ❒ Playing at the beach
- ❒ Dancing
- ❒ Gymnastics
- ❒ Climbing trees
- ❒ Playing hopscotch
- ❒ Walking
- ❒ Running
- ❒ Walking the dog
- ❒ Helping clean the house
- ❒ Rugby
- ❒ Lacrosse
- ❒ Flag football
- ❒ ____________________
- ❒ ____________________

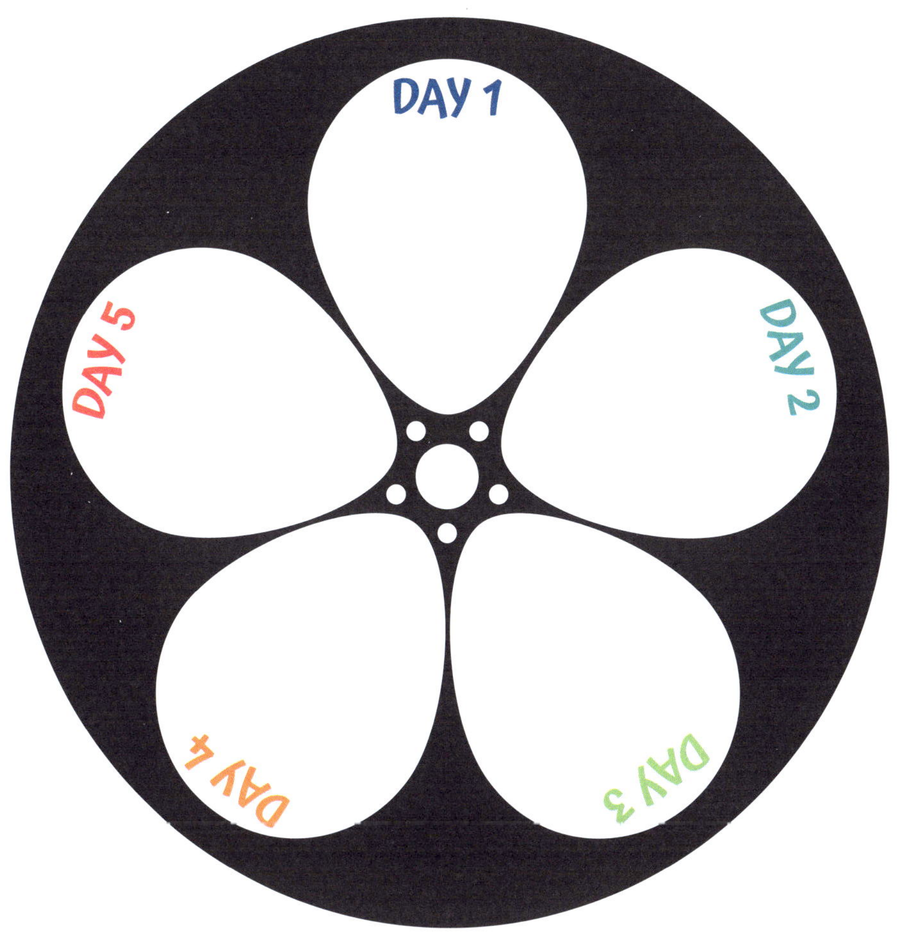

Pick one exercise to DO and one healthy food to EAT every day (for 5 days). In the wheel above, write down your picks.

For example: Day 1, walk for 30 minutes and eat a bowl of cherries. Day 2, ride your bike and put cucumber in your salad.

Creating a healthy routine starts with TODAY! But don't stop at 5 days. Getting exercise and eating healthy are both good habits, just like brushing your teeth. Plan ways you can be healthy every day.

MUSIC PLAYLIST

SONGS

It's proven that upbeat music can make you feel happier!

Make a list of songs that **make you feel good!** They can be songs that make you smile, songs that make you feel energetic, or songs that simply put you in a good mood. Can you create a music playlist? Perhaps ask your parents or guardians for help with this task.

"If music be the food of love, play on."

William Shakespeare

SPECIAL TASK

Fellow music lover, here's what I want you to do. For the next 5 days, listen to your playlist from the page before. Before you listen, rate your mood on a scale from 1 to 10 (with 1 being a not-so-good mood and 10 being a GREAT mood!). After you're done listening, rate your mood again, and see if the music made any difference in how you feel.

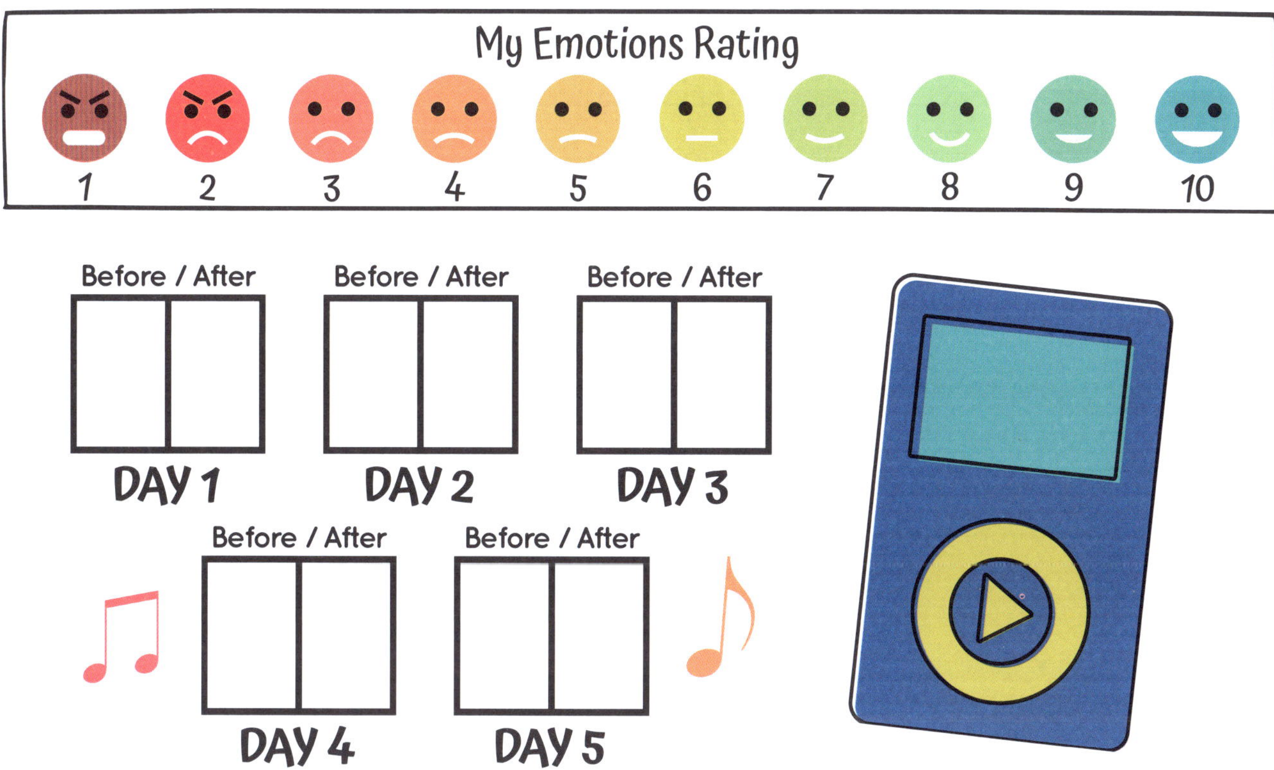

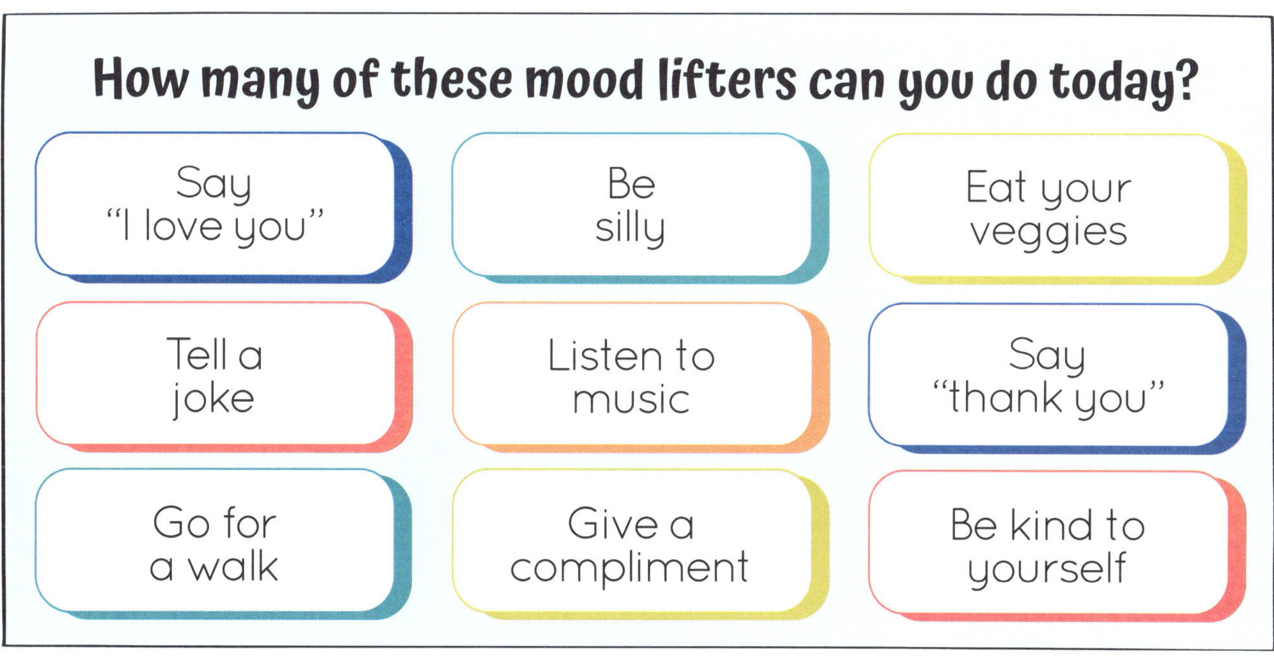

SECRET INGREDIENTS FOR HAPPINESS

PG-13

When people think about happiness, they tend to focus on "stuff," like toys, candy, or video games. But here's the thing: The happiness you feel over stuff quickly fades. Toys, candy, and video games are all great things, but for this exercise, let's look a little deeper. You might find that the real source of your happiness isn't what it seems.

FOR EXAMPLE

When you think about summertime, I bet you remember having a family fun-filled day at the beach or the exhilaration of an adventurous family bike ride.

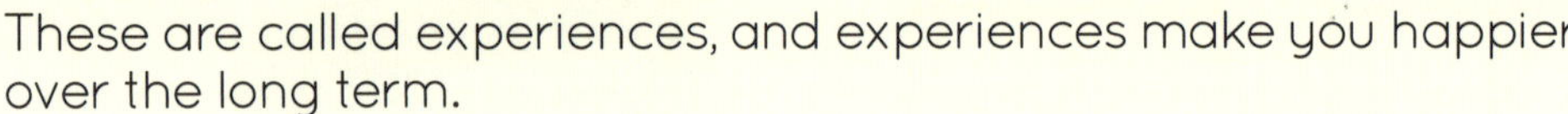

These are called experiences, and experiences make you happier over the long term.

Describe 3 of your own special experiences from this year below.

Think about memorable moments, like a family celebration, a paddleboat ride with someone you love, or the time you shared a joke (and a laugh) with a friend.

Name 3 people who make you feel happy:

Happiness Crossword Puzzle

Answer the fun questions below to fill in the blanks in the puzzle.

ACROSS

A These are often called man's best friend.

B I love to sing Happy _________ to others on their special day.

C Beings from outer space.

D A frozen treat on a hot day.

DOWN

1 Pools of water that I love jumping in on rainy days.

2 Long and lazy summer ____.

3 Floating party decorations at birthday parties.

4 It's yellow and high in the sky, and it makes us warm while we're outside.

5 Who doesn't love a sock ______ show?

** TOP SECRET **
ANSWER KEY
Across
A: Dogs
B: Birthday
C: Aliens
D: Popsicle
Down
1: Puddles
2: Days
3: Balloons
4: Sun
5: Puppet
PUDDLES
DOGS
DAYS
BIRTHDAY
BALLOONS
ALIENS
SUN
PUPPET
POPSICLE

HAPPINESS AND ME

Here you can write freely about what happiness is and what makes you happy!

Let's go:

Stuck on what to write about? Here are a few ideas:

What instantly boosts your mood?

What makes you laugh?

What makes you smile?

Who makes you feel good?

If you had a secret rocket ship and could travel anywhere in the universe, where would you go?

Draw yourself on a rocket ship below!

MISSION REPORT

When you grow up, what job do you think would make you happy?

Describe your happiest family memory:

Describe your happiest school memory:

Circle how you feel right now:

sad

confused

neutral

upset

happy

playful

"HAPPINESS IS THE ONLY THING THAT MULTIPLIES WHEN YOU SHARE IT!"

Albert Schweitzer

Certificate of Completion

This certificate is presented to special agent:

for completing the top-secret training mission:

CHASE DOWN HAPPINESS

Presented by: The Amazing Me Academy

MISSION 7

EXPLORE YOUR STRENGTHS

COMPLETE ALL THE ASSIGNMENTS IN MISSION "EXPLORE YOUR STRENGTHS" TO RECEIVE YOUR NEXT SPECIAL AGENT CERTIFICATE!

LET'S GROW STRONG!

Did you know you have hidden strengths?

Everyone has things they are good at. Sometimes you might recognize your strengths instantly, like "I'm so good at soccer" or "I'm a pro at making fart noises." And other times, your strengths might not be so noticeable. For example, you might be someone who is always helpful or kind, and believe me, that IS a strength. In this mission we'll shine a flashlight on ALL your strengths, and then you can make them even stronger!

Did you know you are growing and changing all the time?

Every living thing grows: plants, trees, animals, and yes, you too! Our bodies grow, and our brains do too. You are constantly learning new things.

Your mindset is a collection of thoughts about how you view yourself and the world around you. Your mindset shapes how you think, feel, and behave.

A **fixed mindset** is the belief that everything about you is frozen and never able to thaw or change. And this simply isn't true. A fixed mindset limits you.

A **growth mindset** is the belief that with hard work and effort, you can achieve your goals. A growth mindset can lead to big and amazing things.

What mindset do you have?

MISSION NOTES

BIG LIST OF STRENGTHS

I am...

- ❒ Honest
- ❒ An expert at making fart noises
- ❒ Helpful
- ❒ Curious
- ❒ Independent
- ❒ A good friend
- ❒ Good at sharing with others
- ❒ Able to get along with others
- ❒ Funny
- ❒ Good with numbers
- ❒ Skilled at strategy games (like chess)
- ❒ A great planner
- ❒ Good at following rules
- ❒ Able to learn from my mistakes
- ❒ A problem solver
- ❒ A team player
- ❒ Artistic or creative
- ❒ Good with technology
- ❒ Athletic
- ❒ An animal lover
- ❒ A good role model for younger kids
- ❒ Musically talented
- ❒ Sensible (people come to me for advice)
- ❒ Brave or courageous
- ❒ Thoughtful
- ❒ A great fort builder
- ❒ Skilled at cooking
- ❒ An avid reader
- ❒ Good at cheering people up
- ❒ Good at making boring things fun

Put a check mark by all your strengths. These are all the things you already do well.

Now look at the items you **didn't** check off. Pick 2 that you'd like to improve:

List the steps you will take to improve these qualities:

Always keep IMPROVING!

INNER STRENGTHS

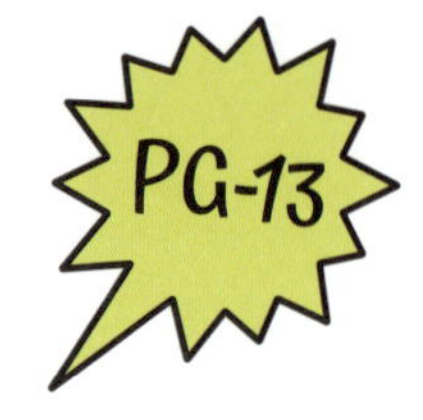

Being strong isn't always about who has the biggest muscles, who is the toughest, or who wins all the time. Strength comes in so many shapes and sizes. There is no one-size-fits-all type of strength.

Being strong is also about your *inner strengths,* like never giving up, having a caring heart, being brave, or overcoming obstacles. When you find yourself in a difficult situation, your inner strengths will pop out. For example, if you're taking a difficult math test, your inner strength of never giving up will pop up and help you finish the test.

You can stop the tug-of-war inside yourself by accepting you for you, big or small, and by focusing on your inner strengths.

Who is a hero to you?

What inner strengths do you think they have?

Draw your hero:

Which of their strengths do you see in yourself?

CHALLENGES TEST YOUR STRENGTHS

GOT PROBLEMS? NO PROBLEM. PROBLEMS ARE REALLY JUST CHALLENGES IN DISGUISE.

Read the common kid-challenges below, and in the boxes to the right, write down what strengths you could grow to overcome these challenges.

YOUR MAZE OF STRENGTH

A maze is a perfect example of how even when you take wrong turns, you can succeed if you keep trying!

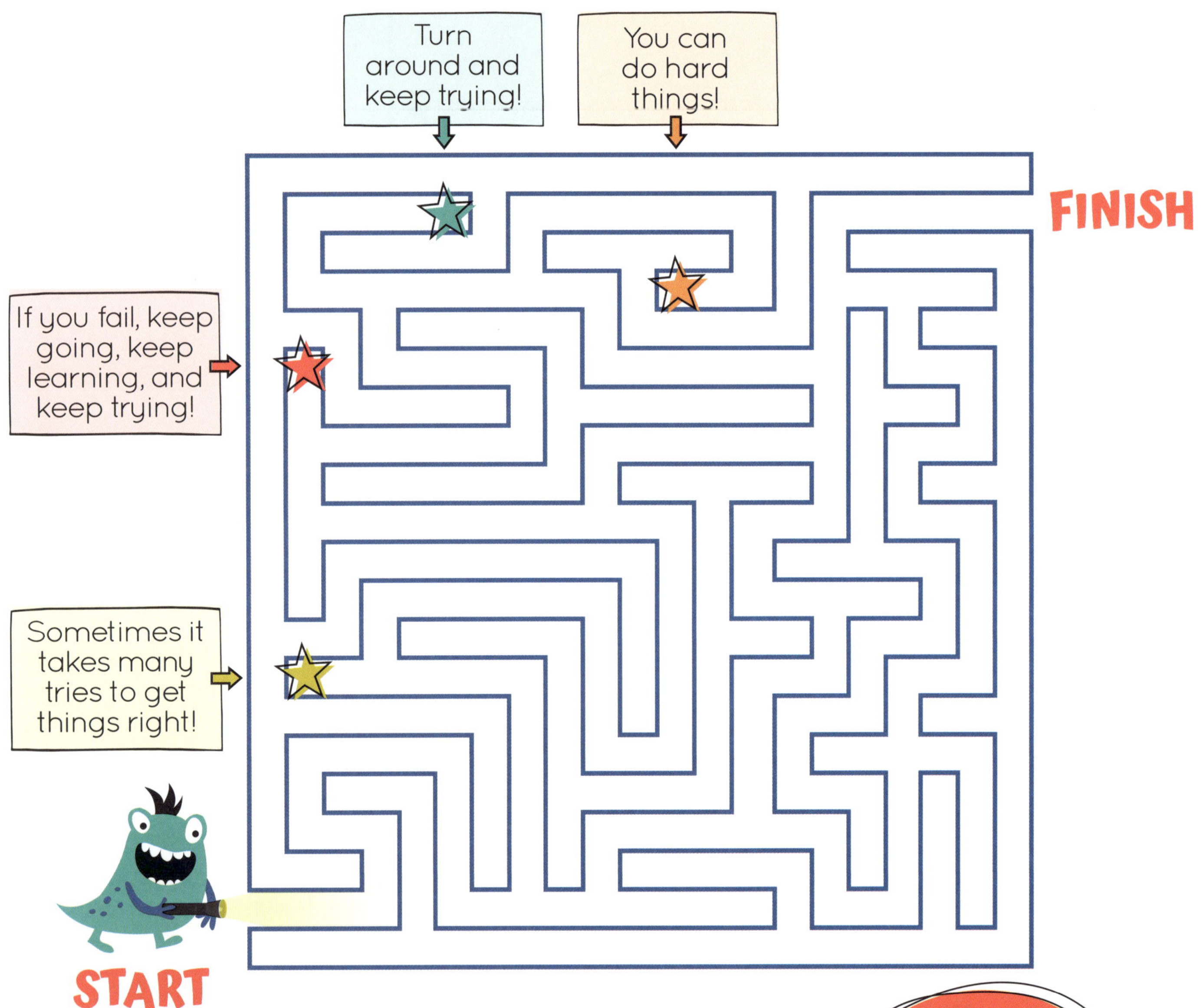

FOCUS ON WHERE YOU ARE RIGHT NOW

In life, there are times when you will fall, get hurt, or fail, but you must get back up and keep trying.

"No one is perfect—that's why pencils have erasers."
Wolfgang Riebe

EVERYBODY MAKES MISTAKES

Everyone makes mistakes—even people you might think never make mistakes, like your teachers, coaches, or parents/guardians.

It's important to admit when you make a mistake instead of trying to hide it. Most mistakes can be fixed.

Sometimes mistakes can even be funny, like when you don't tighten the orange juice lid and your brother spills it all over! Sometimes mistakes are serious, and you might need help from an adult. And usually, mistakes aren't as bad as you think.

Ask your parent or guardian to tell you about a time they made a mistake. Ask them to describe how they handled this situation and what they learned from the experience.

Describe a mistake you have made and how you learned from it.

Write down only the facts, without any excuses or explanations. An example of an excuse would be: "I hit my sister because she hit me first." Just explain your part in this mistake.

"As long as we live, we will never make enough mistakes not to learn, and we will never learn enough not to make mistakes."

Azwindini Mulaudzi

A STORY OF STRENGTH

SHAQUEM GRIFFIN

FUN FACTS:

Shaquem played football in college, and when he graduated in 2017, he was drafted by the Seattle Seahawks.

He is the first one-handed player to play in the NFL!

He has a twin brother who also plays professional football!

DON'T LET ANYONE TELL YOU THAT YOU CAN'T DO SOMETHING YOU BELIEVE IN.

Because of a very rare medical condition, Shaquem only has one hand. Despite this challenge, he started playing football at 5 years old. He also played baseball and competed in track.

WOW!

Griffin was named 1 of 2 recipients of the 2019 NCAA Inspiration Award, which is presented to individuals in the athletic field who have shown especially inspirational efforts in dealing with difficult situations.

Shaquem is an inspiration to encourage everyone to follow their dreams.

Shaquem is an inspiration to kids everywhere. He is someone who never quit and achieved BIG things. Sometimes life is hard, but if you keep trying and keep working, you can accomplish anything.

"Nobody was ever going to tell me that I didn't belong on a football field. And nobody was ever going to tell me that I couldn't be great."

Shaquem Griffin

WHAT STRENGTHS DO YOU THINK SHAQUEM HAS?

WHAT CAN YOU LEARN FROM SHAQUEM?

HAVE YOU EVER FACED ANYTHING REALLY TOUGH, WHERE YOU MIGHT HAVE FELT DIFFERENT OR LEFT OUT?

FAILURE IS IMPORTANT

Yes, you read that correctly!

- Failure can make you dig deep and find the strength to try again.
- Failure helps you develop new and better ways of doing things that you haven't thought of yet.
- Failure means you actually tried something!
- Failure gives you valuable life experience and helps you grow.

NAME A TIME YOU'VE TRIED SOMETHING AND FAILED
(THINK ABOUT WHAT THIS TAUGHT YOU)

"THE ONLY REAL MISTAKE IS THE ONE FROM WHICH WE LEARN NOTHING."

Henry Ford

BUILDING ON MY STRENGTHS, ONE STEP AT A TIME

Think of something you're pretty good at but want to get better at. Describe it below:

It can be anything! Maybe you want to improve your grades from "okay" to "excellent," learn a new dance step, or take on a new challenge in a video game you've been playing.

What steps will you take to get there?

When you fall down, what can you do to get back up and try again?

Now imagine yourself succeeding. What does it feel like?

MISSION REPORT

What have you learned about yourself during this mission?

Did anything you learned about yourself surprise you?

Describe the bravest thing you've ever done:

Describe how you feel after you accomplish something really hard:

"Nothing can dim the light which shines from within."

Maya Angelou

Certificate of Completion

This certificate is presented to special agent:

for completing the top-secret training mission:

EXPLORE YOUR STRENGTHS

Presented by: The Amazing Me Academy

MISSION 8

CONFIDENCE CADET

COMPLETE ALL THE ASSIGNMENTS IN MISSION "CONFIDENCE CADET" TO RECEIVE YOUR NEXT SPECIAL AGENT CERTIFICATE!

YOU ARE ONE OF A KIND

This mission is all about becoming a confidence cadet!

In the previous mission, you identified your strengths. Now it's time to help you really believe in how great you are.

Here's the thing: You can't be good at everything. Chances are you'll likely be downright terrible at some things. And of course, some things you'll do like a total rock star. You are you.

Famous musicians or pro sports players are incredible at what they do, but remember: They have spent oodles of time perfecting their talents. And that famous musician might be a total klutz when it comes to sports. No one is good at everything.

Being a confidence cadet is about appreciating the awesomeness in others AND in yourself. But sometimes, it can be tricky to realize your own awesomeness.

Let's stop wishing to be something we aren't and start being ourselves!

REMEMBER: You are FULL of endless potential.

MISSION NOTES

Use 5 words to describe yourself to someone who doesn't know you:

What is the best compliment you've ever received?

What do you like best about your personality?

What's your favorite physical feature?

POSITIVE SELF-TALK

Thoughts are a bit like dandelions in the spring: They pop up all the time! Many of these thoughts are happy thoughts (like thinking about your favorite ice cream flavor or your cute new puppy). But some of these thoughts are not happy (like telling yourself you won't ever be able to ride a bike or learn your math tables). These negative thoughts bring us down.

HERE'S THE THING:

Negative thoughts aren't always true or useful. Below, write down any nagging negative thoughts you keep having, then rewrite the thought in a positive way.

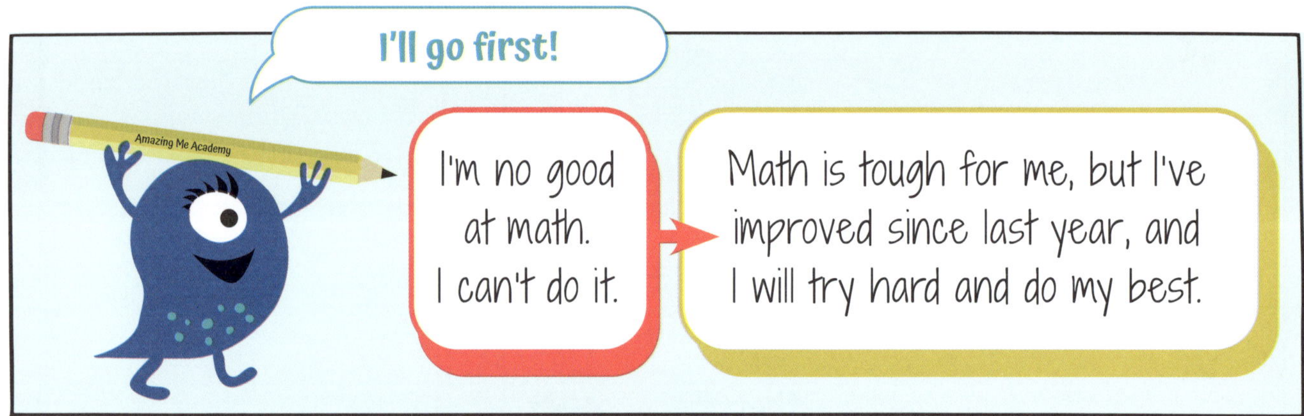

Now it's your turn!

Nagging negative thought:	Positive thought:
Nagging negative thought:	Positive thought:
Nagging negative thought:	Positive thought:

TRY NEW THINGS

Think about all the things that were once new, scary, or difficult that now seem easy. Go on, try something new! What's the worst that could happen?

- Would you like to learn to ride a horse?
- Play a musical instrument?
- Eat brussels sprouts?
- Make a lemonade stand?
- Go camping in the backyard?

DON'T BE AFRAID TO TRY NEW THINGS.

TODAY WE ARE GOING ON AN ADVENTURE!

3 new things I want to try:

☆ ____________________

☆ ____________________

☆ ____________________

REMEMBER

"All your dreams can come true if you have the courage to pursue them."

Walt Disney

STANDING UP FOR YOURSELF...

1. Learn to identify when something feels off

Conflict is when we disagree with someone. This is bound to happen because we all have different personalities and opinions. Learn to recognize the signs in your body that you are feeling uncomfortable: You might feel scared, become fidgety, or have butterflies in your stomach. Your face might grow red, and your stomach might get upset.

2. Know your boundaries

Boundaries are emotional and physical lines that other people shouldn't cross. You need to set boundaries. When someone is doing something you don't like, whether it's giving an unwanted hug or teasing you, practice using stop words like "Stop that" or "No!"

3. Use "I" statements

Sometimes when we disagree with others, they can feel like we're attacking and blaming them. One way to prevent others from feeling criticized is to use "I" statements. Here are some examples of "I" statements:

"I feel angry when you interrupt me because it makes me feel like my words don't matter."

"I feel embarrassed when you kiss me in front of my friends. They tease me."

Make up your own "I" statement the next time a problem arises.

4. Role-play with your grown-ups, siblings, or friends

The key to mastering any skill is to practice, practice, practice. Ask a trusted friend or grown-up to role-play with you. Think of this as a unique game of charades. Consider a difficult situation. Perhaps a classmate is picking on you. Practice your responses so you'll know what to do when and if the situation happens in real life.

Remember to always listen to others, and think carefully before responding.

The Ultimate Battle of Thoughts

Let's have a duel with our thoughts! Who will win?

When you have an upsetting thought, there are several questions you can ask yourself that will challenge whether this thought is true. Write your upsetting thought in the circle below, and then ask yourself the questions presented in the clouds.

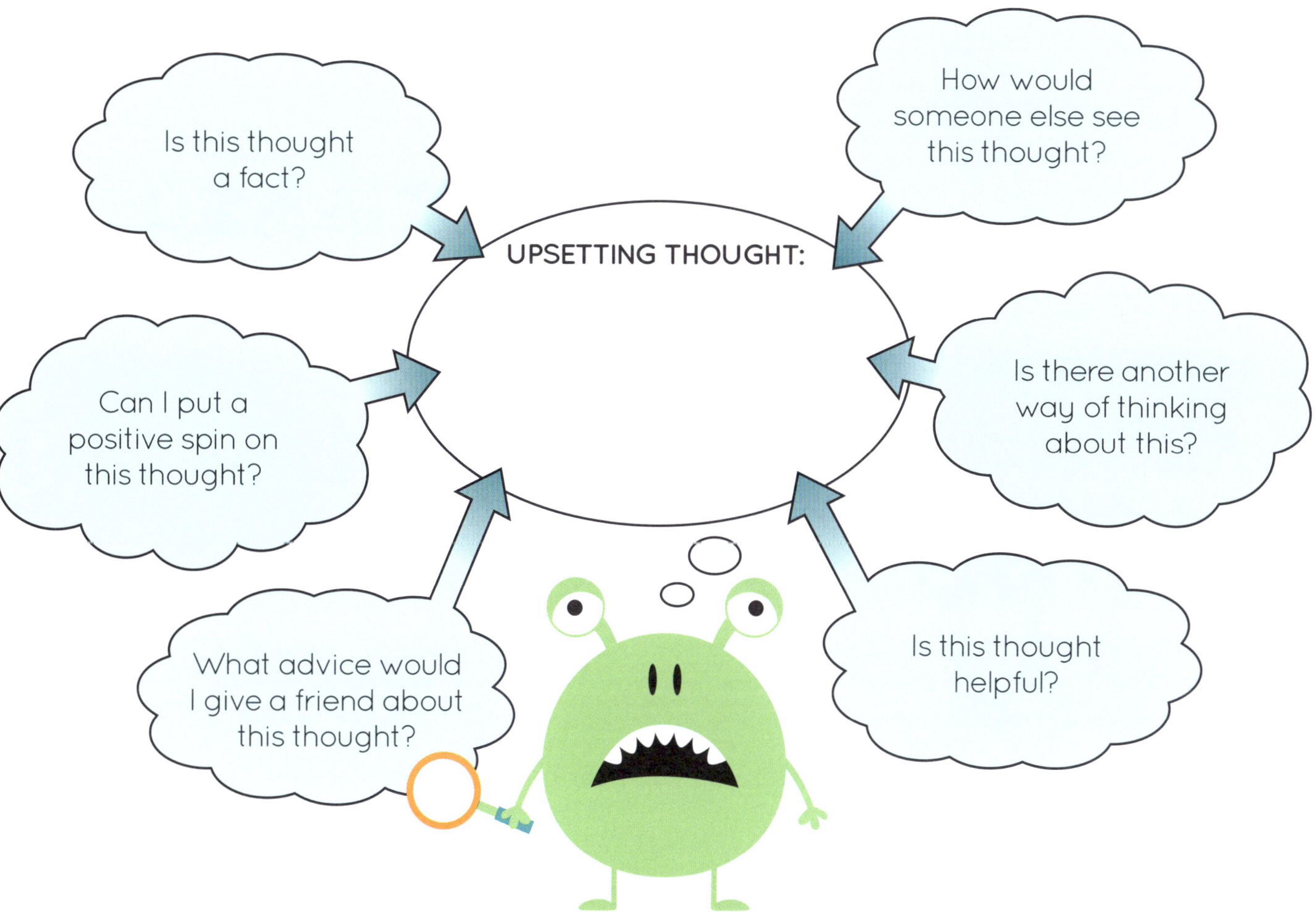

When people say mean things about us, it hurts! But remember, everyone has an opinion, and others won't always like us or agree with us.

If something feels too big or tough, or if someone is bullying you or making you feel bad, talk to a trusted adult. Help is available.

Did you know that others are NOT thinking about you nearly as much as you think they are? Other people are often worried about what YOU think about them. Remember this the next time you feel like others are judging you.

TAKE CARE OF YOU

Did you know routines increase your confidence?

I'm totally serious. You might think routines are more boring than watching paint dry, but routines actually make you feel safe and help you handle anything life might throw your way. Routines help you tackle change and challenges, like walking to school by yourself, making your own bed, or preparing your own lunch. These things make it easier to be a confidence cadet!

"What you do every day matters more than what you do once in a while."

Gretchen Rubin

MY BEDTIME ROUTINE

CREATE NEW HABITS

For the next 5 days, try out these 2 new habits: Every morning, make your bed, and every evening, put away any toys on the floor of your room. Put a check mark below as you complete these tasks each day.

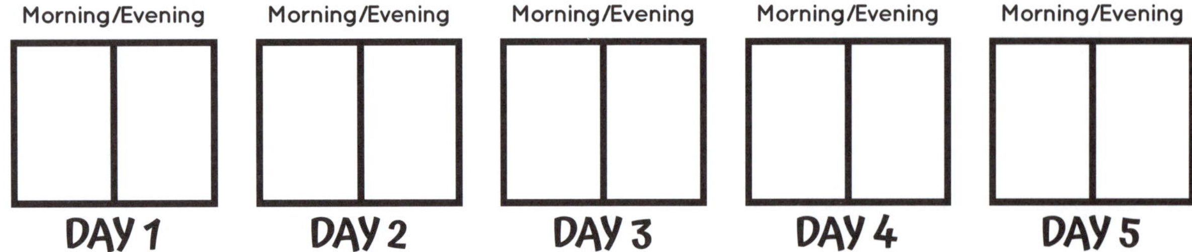

POSITIVE AFFIRMATIONS

Affirmations are positive statements we tell ourselves to help us feel stronger and more confident. If you're new to affirmations, it can feel a little silly. Okay, maybe A LOT silly. But this silly habit has ENORMOUS benefits. Saying and thinking positive things is like having a thought teleportation machine. Affirmations teleport negative thoughts away and give you happy thoughts to focus on instead.

Here are some examples of affirmations: *"I feel calm." "I am loved." "I am safe." "I will be kind to everyone." "I love myself and my life." "I believe in myself and the people around me."*

Repeat these affirmations until your thought teleportation machine replaces your negative thoughts with positive ones.

THE SKY'S THE LIMIT	IF I BELIEVE IT, I CAN ACHIEVE IT	I'M ONE SMART COOKIE
I CAN CHOOSE TO HAVE A GREAT DAY	CHALLENGES MAKE ME STRONGER	THERE IS ONLY ONE ME, AND I AM SPECIAL
I HAVE THE COURAGE TO FACE MY FEARS	I FEEL CALM AND PEACEFUL	I AM LOVED

Don't limit yourself to these affirmations. Say anything that makes you feel good!

MISSION REPORT

Are there things you can do to continue building your confidence in the days and weeks that follow?

What color best represents your personality?

What's something nice you could say to yourself?

What do you wish your grown-ups or friends knew about you?

Imagine yourself in 5 years. What are you most excited for?

"ALWAYS,
always,
always
BELIEVE
in
YOURSELF."

Marilyn Monroe

Certificate of Completion

This certificate is presented to special agent:

for completing the top-secret training mission:

CONFIDENCE CADET

Presented by: The Amazing Me Academy

MISSION 9

GOAL GETTER

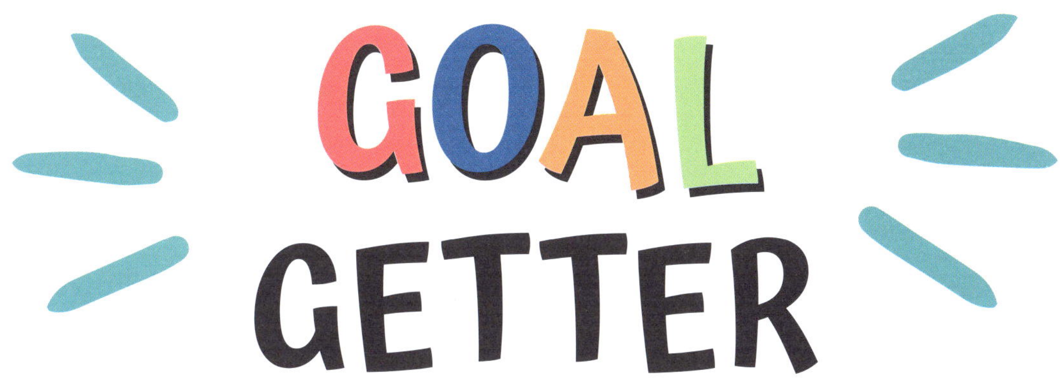

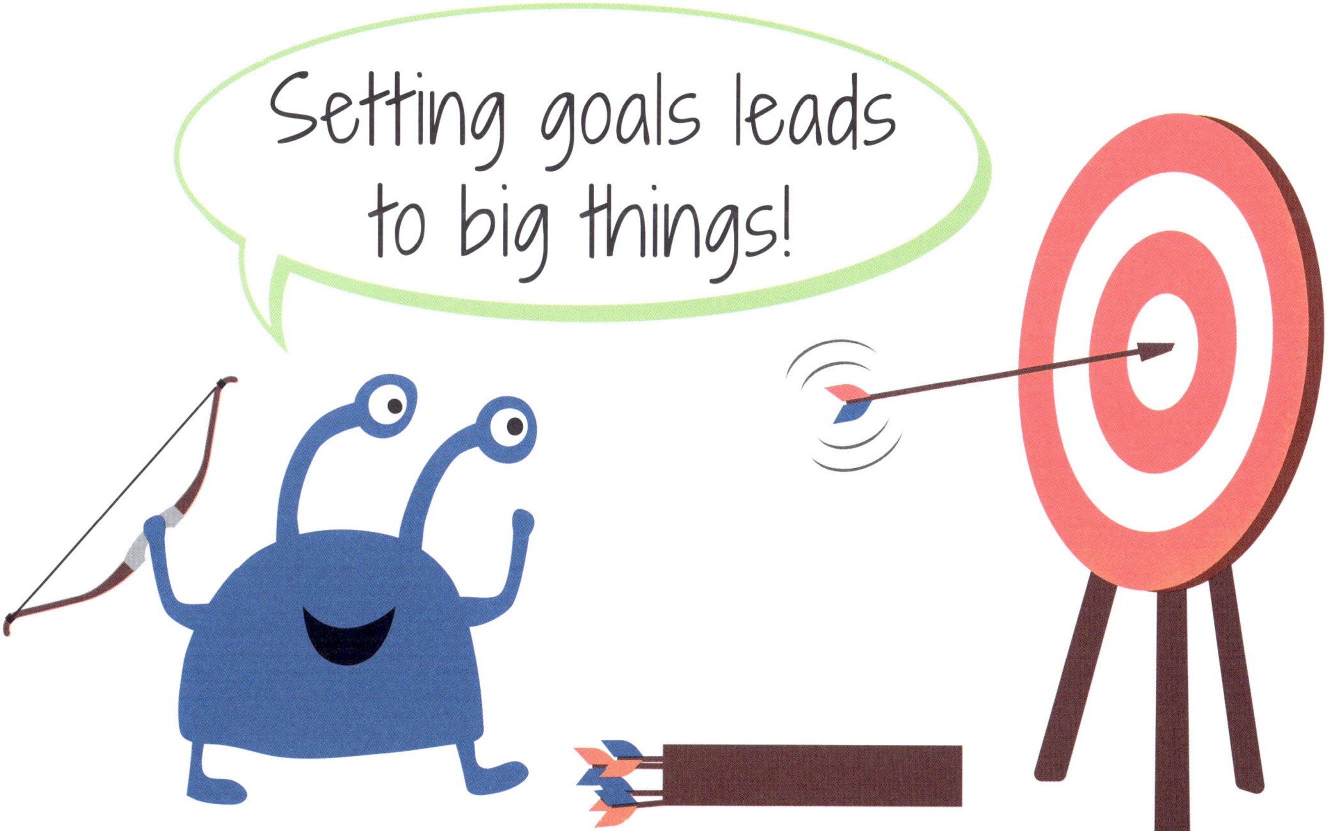
Setting goals leads to big things!

COMPLETE ALL THE ASSIGNMENTS IN MISSION "GOAL GETTER" TO RECEIVE YOUR NEXT SPECIAL AGENT CERTIFICATE!

YOUR GOALS MATTER

This mission is all about setting goals.

Goal setting is an important habit (especially at your age). It keeps you moving forward and keeps you growing as a person. You can set tiny goals or great big goals. Either way, go get 'em!

Setting a SMART goal is an easy way to break down a goal into tiny steps. Doing so makes it more likely that you will succeed.

Specific

Your goal should be clear and sensible, and it should state exactly what you want. For example, "I want to do better in school" is an unclear and vague goal, but "I want to be able to recite my times tables from 1 to 10 without making any mistakes" is very clear and specific.

Measurable

Think about how you'll know when you've reached your goal. How will you know you've succeeded? For example, will you achieve your goal when you can easily recite your times tables from 1 to 10?

Achievable

Is your goal achievable? As much as you might want to learn how to fly, is that realistic? Daydreaming is terrific, but when you're setting a goal, make sure there are steps you can take to achieve it.

Relevant

Relevant is another word for important. So, ask yourself: Is this really your goal? Does your goal matter to you? Take care to ensure it's not just what someone else wants you to do. Is it the right time to set this goal? Is it worthwhile? If your answer is "Heck yeah, I want to learn my times tables so I can be a mathematical rock star in school," then it's a relevant goal.

Timebound

Goals need an end date. Is this a goal you will complete in a few days or one that might take a few weeks or even months?

MISSION NOTES

What would you do if you knew you'd succeed?

Draw it:

Write a positive affirmation to repeat to yourself during this mission:

"A goal without a plan is just a wish."

Antoine de Saint-Exupéry

BRAINSTORMING GOALS

Maybe you'd like to...

- Try a new sport?
- Get a certain grade?
- Read a certain book?
- Learn how to cook, play a musical instrument, dance, sing, or draw?
- Talk out of turn less in class?
- Do 3 kind things for someone this week?
- Learn about the planets or oceans?
- Share more?
- Get to bed by a certain time each night?
- Get 1 hour of exercise each day?
- Make the best paper airplane?
- Swim underwater?
- Try 3 new foods this week?
- Learn your times tables?
- Visit a waterfall this year?
- Make dinner all on your own?
- Learn 10 yoga poses?
- Earn a reward or a medal?

Read the prompts to the left and start to think about all the different goals you could set for yourself (big and small). Below, jot down your ideas.

LOOK, now you have an entire sheet of goals you can pull from!

"You'll always miss 100% of the shots you don't take."

Wayne Gretzky

From the goals below, place a check mark beside examples of good SMART goal statements and an X beside any not-so-good goal statements.

I want to do better in school.	I want to learn my mathematical times tables by the end of next month.
I want to get better at tae kwon do.	I will practice tae kwon do 3 times a week for the next month.
I will spend less time on screens.	I will use a timer to limit my screen time to 1 hour each day for the next 30 days. Then I will reevaluate.

As you can see, the goals on the right-hand side are specific, achievable, and have a set time frame (they are SMART goals). The goals on the left are very general. This makes it very hard to complete these goals.

Try setting goals in different areas of your life

There are many different types of goals you can set that will open up different areas of your life to new and exciting things. For example, your goal might be to help with chores at home, learn calm-down strategies, or practice baseball every day.

Family goal	**Physical goal**	**School goal**
Hobby goal	**Personal goal**	**Emotional goal**

MY BIG GOAL

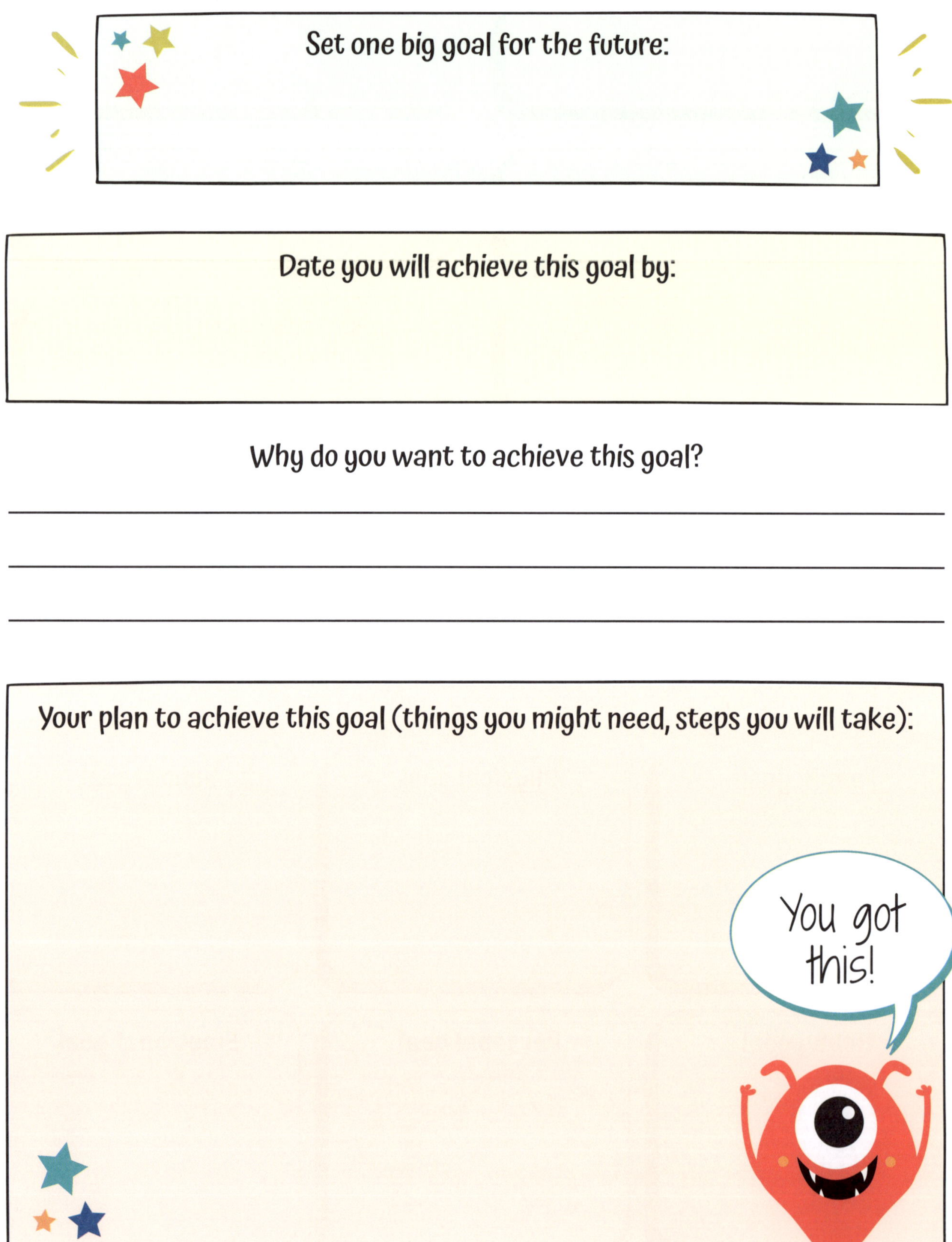

Set one big goal for the future:
Date you will achieve this goal by:
Why do you want to achieve this goal?
Your plan to achieve this goal (things you might need, steps you will take):
You got this!

OVERCOMING OBSTACLES

Obstacles may come up that might stand in your way of achieving your big goal. But this is not the time to give up.

List 3 obstacles that might come up and how you will overcome them.

1.

2.

3.

How you'll feel when you achieve your big goal:

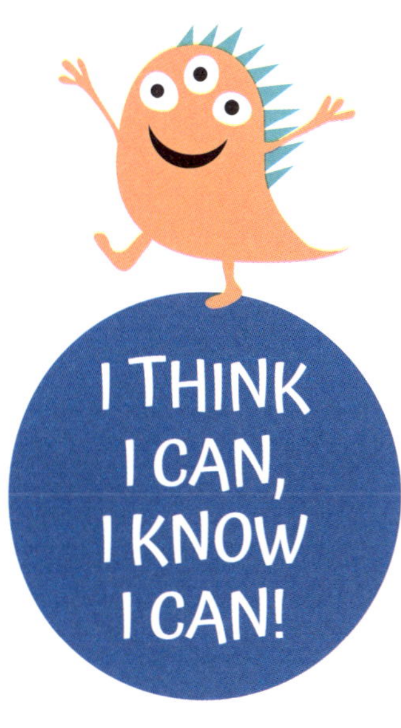

THE POWER OF GOAL SETTING

GRETA THUNBERG

GRETA THUNBERG IS AN AMAZING YOUNG WOMAN!

Greta was born in Sweden and first learned about climate change when she was only 8. Greta would like to see all of us take care of the planet and take climate change seriously!

GRETA SAYS,

"You are never too small to make a difference."

BIG NEWS

In 2019, when she was just 16 years old, Greta was named *Time* magazine's Person of the Year. Greta is the youngest person to ever receive this award.

She was also labeled *Time*'s most influential teen of 2018, nominated for the Nobel Peace Prize in 2019, and listed in *Time*'s 100 most influential people in the world that year. **And the list of awards and recognition goes on from there.**

FUN FACTS:

Greta Thunberg has become world-famous for her work on climate change.

Greta has inspired over 4 million people to join the global climate movement.

Greta is also encouraging others like her who have high-functioning autism to follow their dreams.

Newspapers around the world have called her effect on the world the "Greta Effect."

WOW!

Greta has high-functioning autism, and she calls this her superpower! While this condition can make things challenging, she focuses on the ways it's also a strength.

"It's quite hilarious when the only thing people can do is mock you, or talk about your appearance or personality, as it means they have no argument or nothing else to say."

Greta Thunberg

Greta certainly had a goal, set her sights on it, worked hard, and made an enormous impact across the world.

What is something you believe strongly in, like Greta?

What SMART (specific, measurable, achievable, relevant, and timebound) steps can you take to work toward this cause?

What are some obstacles that might arise? How could you overcome them?

SKOLSTREJK FÖR KLIMATET

Goal Word Search

How many words can you find that relate to goal setting?

d s e n w i s h h g h b
o u a m b i t i o n u e
d c f x i q a s p d c l
r c p l a n r c e e j i
e e k p n s t e p s m e
a e l t d f y q k i p v
m d w g r u s t o r y e
a o t f x n y b m e p u
m i s s i o n z l s f z

I found 13 words!

TASK

Choose any 2 of the words you found, and use them in a sentence below.

** TOP SECRET **

ANSWER KEY

1. wish
2. succeed
3. can
4. ambition
5. hope
6. step
7. fun
8. mission
9. desire
10. story
11. believe
12. plan
13. start

d	s	e	n	w	i	s	h	h	g	h	b
o	u	a	m	b	i	t	i	o	n	u	e
d	c	f	x	i	q	a	s	p	d	c	l
r	c	p	l	a	n	r	c	e	e	j	i
e	e	k	p	n	s	t	e	p	s	m	e
a	e	l	t	d	f	y	q	k	i	p	v
m	d	w	g	r	u	s	t	o	r	y	e
a	o	t	f	x	n	y	b	m	e	p	u
m	i	s	s	i	o	n	z	l	s	f	z

MAKING CHANGE

Think of habits you might have that are not helping you be happy and succeed. These could be habits such as arguing, not being kind, being hard on yourself, not taking care of your things, or being unhelpful. Could you let go of these habits? And could you replace them with healthy habits? Below are 3 examples of not-so-helpful habits replaced by 3 helpful habits.

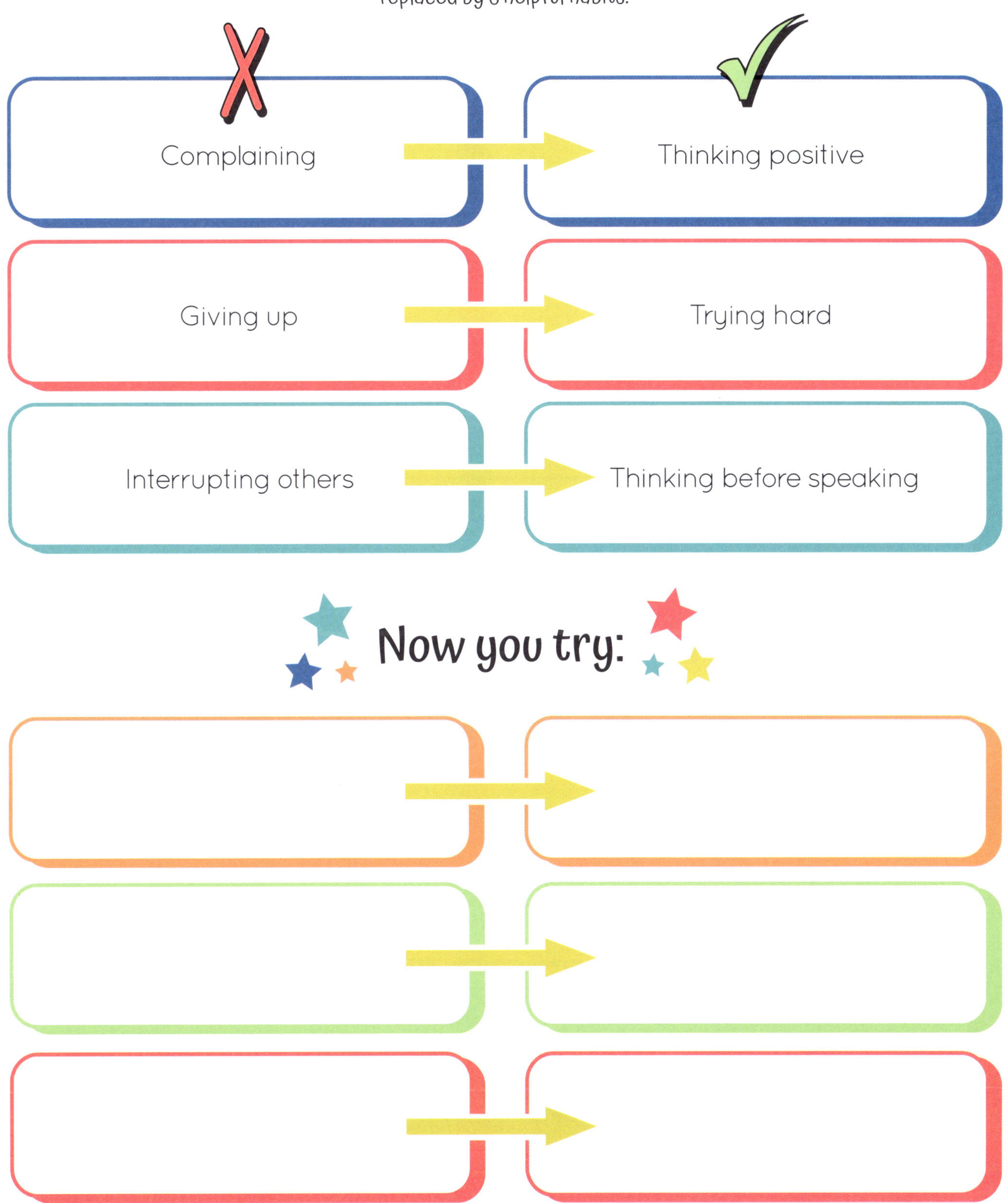

MISSION REPORT

What accomplishment are you proudest of?

If you could be anything, what would it be?

Describe 3 things you have always wanted to try:

1.

2.

3.

"There is only one thing that makes a dream impossible to achieve: the fear of failure."
Paulo Coelho

"DO WHAT YOU CAN,
WITH WHAT YOU HAVE,
WHERE YOU ARE."

Theodore Roosevelt

Certificate of Completion

This certificate is presented to special agent:

for completing the top-secret training mission:

GOAL GETTER

Presented by: The Amazing Me Academy

MISSION 10

THE POWER OF KINDNESS

Kindness is cool, so spread it wherever you go!

COMPLETE ALL THE ASSIGNMENTS IN MISSION "THE POWER OF KINDNESS" TO RECEIVE YOUR NEXT SPECIAL AGENT CERTIFICATE!

WHY KINDNESS MATTERS

During this mission we will zoom in on how to spread kindness!

It's simple! When you practice kindness, YOU feel good, and so do others. It's important to be kind to everyone, even when it's hard. You can be kind to others, yourself, animals, and the planet.

Kindness can look like:

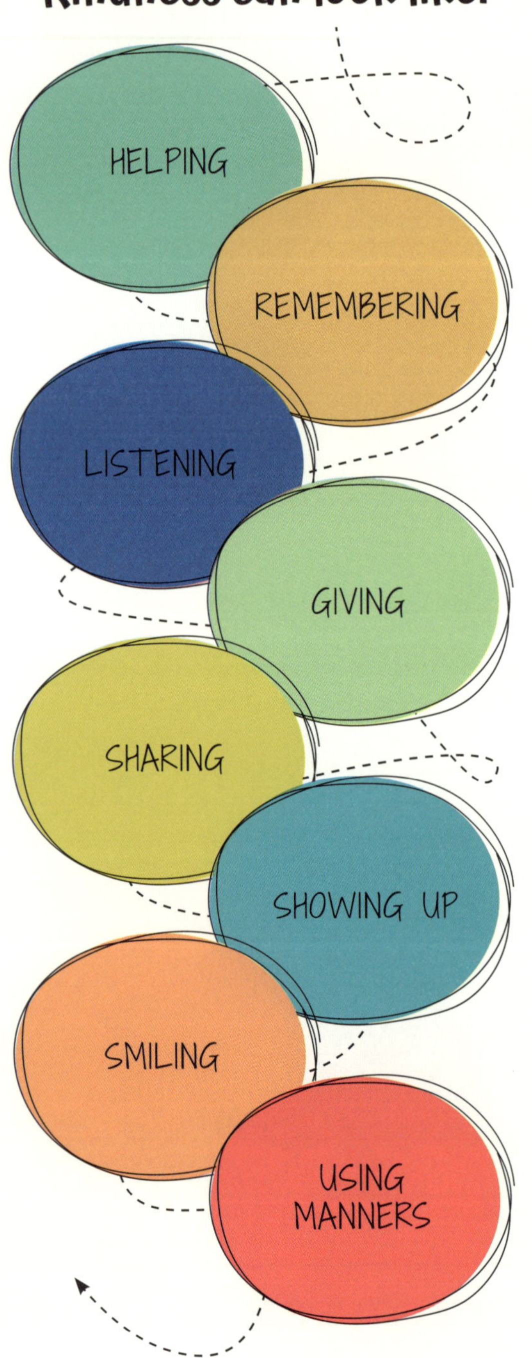

THE BENEFITS OF KINDNESS

- Kindness makes you and others happier.
- Kindness is good for your health.
- Kindness improves relationships.
- Kindness brings people together.
- Kindness spreads around the world.

"Be kind whenever possible. It is always possible."

Dalai Lama

MISSION NOTES

5 ways you can be kind to others:

How does it make you feel when someone is kind to you?

Ways you can be kinder to the planet:

KINDNESS ROCKS

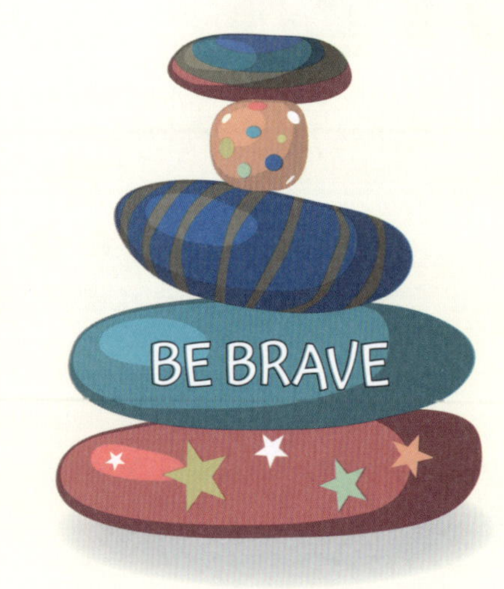

Kindness rocks are a great way to spread joy, kindness, and inspiration. They are rocks that you collect and paint with inspirational messages. You can hide these nuggets of joy for others to find or give them as gifts to special friends or family. Can you imagine the delight on someone's face when they stumble across one of your hidden rocks? This could be just the message they need to turn their day around.

1. Gather Rocks

You can find rocks at a park, beach, or waterfront. You can even purchase them at a craft store.

2. Wash Rocks

Wash your rocks well, and allow them to completely dry. If you want vibrant colors, apply a base coat of white paint.

3. Paint Rocks

Use a brush and non-toxic acrylic craft paint. Paint your background colors first, let them dry, and then write your kindness messages on the rocks. (Stuck? You'll find some ideas on the next page!) Tip: Use a fine- or medium-tip paint marker for your message.

4. Distribute Rocks

This is the REALLY fun part. Hide your rocks in a bunch of different places! The next page includes a list of great places to hide your rocks.

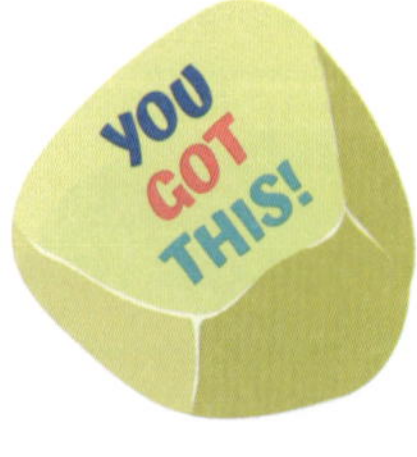

MESSAGE IDEAS FOR ROCKS

Just Breathe	Never Stop Looking Up	Do What Makes Your Soul Shine
You Got This!	Make Today Great	Laugh More!
Life's a Journey, Not a Race	Collect Moments, Not Things	Be Silly, Be Kind, Be Honest
Mistakes Are Proof You Are Trying	Teach, Love, Inspire	Think Happy Thoughts
If You Can Dream It, You Can Do It	You Are Capable of Amazing Things	Be Awesome Today
Say Yes to New Adventures	Be the Reason Someone Smiles Today	Be Your Best Self

Ideas of places to hide your rocks

1. Parks
2. Swimming pools
3. Sidewalks
4. Schoolyard
5. Library bookshelves
6. Splash pad
7. Amusement park or zoo
8. Hiking trails
9. Community center
10. Sports field
11. Beach
12. Around the neighborhood
13. Mall or stores
14. Restaurants
15. Downtown or at the waterfront

THE POWER OF KINDNESS

NELSON MANDELA

Nelson Mandela was an incredibly kind man. He made a difference in the world despite years of challenging times.

FUN FACTS:

Nelson Mandela spent 27 years in prison and, when released, became the first Black President of South Africa!

He had 6 children!

Mandela often used sports to bring people together.

NELSON MANDELA IS THE FACE OF PEACE AND KINDNESS.

Nelson Mandela always stood up for his beliefs. He believed everyone should be treated equally and fairly. But the people in charge of his country did not share his ideas. Even though he protested peacefully, he was arrested and went on to spend 27 years in prison.

Imagine spending 27 years in prison just because you wanted people to be treated fairly.

BUT THAT DIDN'T STOP HIM.

When he was finally released from prison, he went on to stand up for his political beliefs. You'll definitely need help from a grown-up to understand this, but basically, he helped stop a racist political and social system. He went on to win the Nobel Peace Prize! Because of him, all people, regardless of race or color, were allowed to vote in South Africa.

On April 27, 1994, South Africa held its first democratic election. And guess who became president?

NONE OTHER THAN NELSON MANDELA HIMSELF. HE WAS 77 YEARS OLD!

Mandela made enormous changes to his country and the entire world.

One of Nelson Mandela's most incredible strengths was his ability to forgive. Despite everything he'd been through (27 years in prison for simply protesting racism), you might think he'd hold a tiny grudge. But his kind nature always won.

> **"As I walked out the door toward the gate that would lead to my freedom, I knew if I didn't leave my bitterness and hatred behind, I'd still be in prison."**
>
> Nelson Mandela

Why do you think it's difficult to forgive someone who hurt you?

Describe a time you forgave someone:

Describe a time you made a mistake and needed to be forgiven:

Draw a picture of what peace means to you:

SEE THE GOOD IN OTHERS

Did you know that when you start seeing the good in others, you start seeing the good in yourself?

Pick any 2 of your friends, and think about the things that make them great. Perhaps they are honest, funny, hardworking, smart, or kind. Why do you love being around them?

Draw pictures of your friends in the boxes:

FRIEND #1

Your friend's name

This is what I love most about ______

______

______

______

______

FRIEND #2

Your friend's name

This is what I love most about ______

______

______

______

______

What qualities do you love about your friends that also characterize YOU?

What qualities do you love about your friends that you'd like to have more of?

KINDNESS NOTES

Hey cadet,

A great way to be kind is to let other people know that you appreciate them. It can be anyone: a teacher, parent/guardian, friend, or neighbor. Cut out these mini notes and tell them why you think they rock. This is sure to brighten someone's day!

You're the best because...

____

____

____

and because...

____

Thanks for being...

____

You're the best because...

____

____

____

and because...

____

Thanks for being...

____

You're the best because...

____

____

____

and because...

____

Thanks for being...

____

You're the best because...

____

____

____

and because...

____

Thanks for being...

____

ONE ACT OF KINDNESS A DAY

Fold the corner of this page down so you can find it again!

For the next 4 weeks, complete 1 act of kindness each day.

Don't just think about being kind, practice being kind!

MON	TUE	WED	THU	FRI	SAT	SUN
Create kindness rocks	Give away a toy	Your choice! 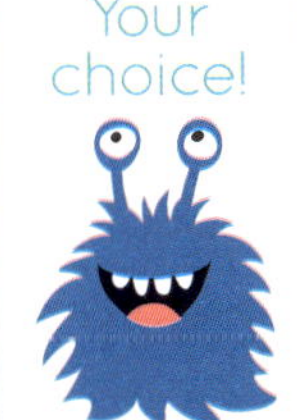	Write down 5 things in your life that you're grateful for	Help your grown-ups with a task	Pick wildflowers for someone	Say something nice to someone
Feed the birds	Make a meal for someone	Bake cookies for 1 lucky person	Your choice! 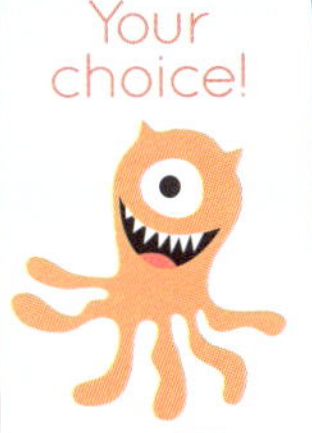	Say 3 positive things to someone today	Leave a note in a book for someone to find	Tell a joke to a friend
Send well-wishes to a friend	Write a thank-you note to your teacher	Write a letter to a loved one	Donate your old books to the library	Your choice! 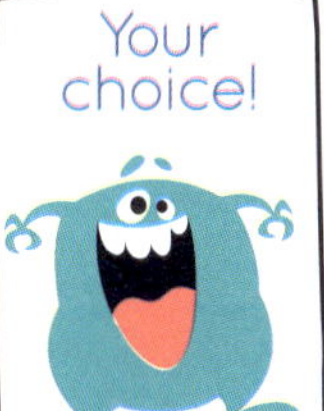	Call a friend to say hello	Tell your parent or caregiver 5 things you love about them
Donate food to your local food bank	Your choice! 	Pick up 10 pieces of litter in a park	Offer hugs to friends or loved ones	Thank people who do things for you	Do something helpful for a family member	Your choice! 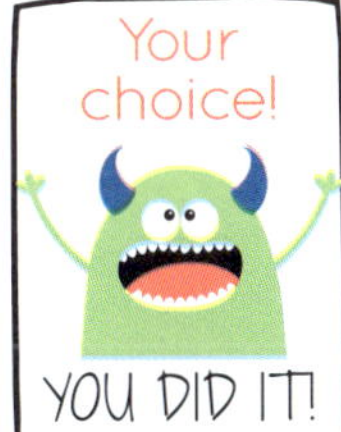 YOU DID IT!

Watch your life change in beautiful ways!

How can your kindness make a difference?

Check off the acts of kindness you have done this year:

- ☐ Plant a tree
- ☐ Recycle
- ☐ Help a friend
- ☐ Give hugs
- ☐ Listen
- ☐ Turn off the lights when you leave
- ☐ Help with chores
- ☐ Pick up litter
- ☐ Don't waste water
- ☐ Prepare a meal for someone
- ☐ Don't waste food
- ☐ Say please and thank you
- ☐ Create something for someone
- ☐ Teach a friend something
- ☐ Donate old toys
- ☐ Donate old clothes
- ☐ Be a good friend
- ☐ Thank your teacher
- ☐ Tell jokes to cheer someone up

Is there more you can do? Brainstorm your ideas here:

CHORE TIME

DID YOU KNOW:

Kids who help with chores have higher self-esteem, are more responsible, and can better cope with frustrations.

Helping with chores will make you feel good! Before you protest and say this is silly—because c'mon, how could doing chores make you feel good?—know that I'm being 100% serious! Helping around the house makes you an essential part of the family. And you are important.

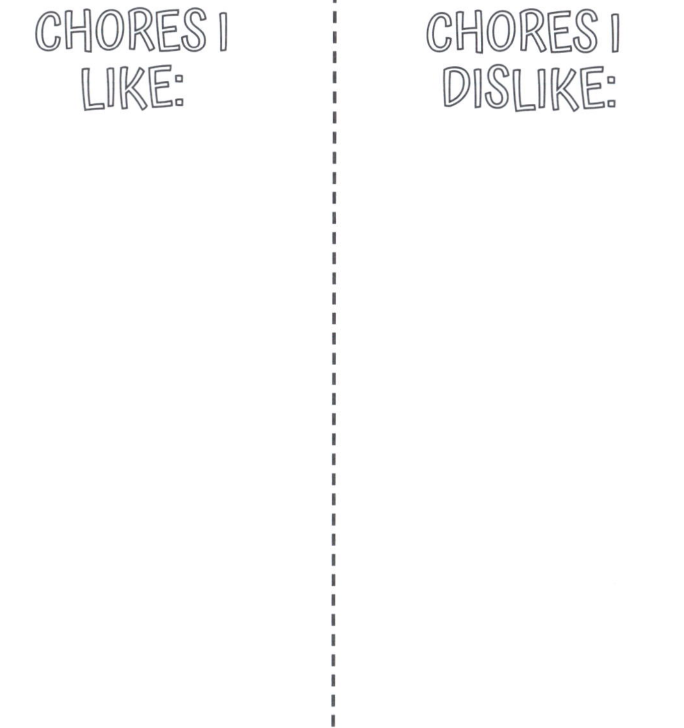

SPECIAL ASSIGNMENT

Pick any 5 chores from your list above, and write 1 chore in each of the boxes below. Each day this week, complete 1 chore and color in the smile face for that day.

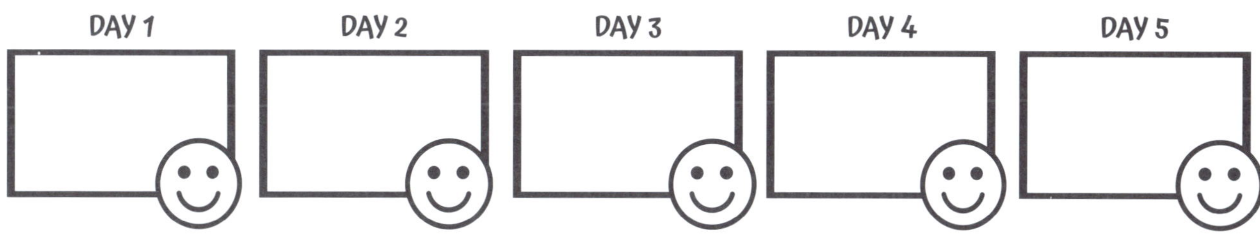

MISSION REPORT

Describe 3 ways you will continue to be kind:

Name 2 people who are kind to you:

This is how kindness feels:

Write down words you use when being kind:

"KINDNESS COSTS NOTHING BUT MEANS EVERYTHING!"

Johnny Stones

Certificate of Completion

This certificate is presented to special agent:

for completing the top-secret training mission:

THE POWER OF KINDNESS

Presented by: The Amazing Me Academy

You've come to the end of Amazing Me!

Look at everything you've learned. You've dabbled in gratitude and mindfulness. You've discovered what makes you happy and how to handle big emotions. You've explored areas of strength and areas for growth. I bet you believe in yourself a little more, and you've maybe even set a few goals. But best of all, you're spreading kindness!

Don't stop here! Be proud and keep learning, growing, and trying your best. Continue to flip back through your journal, read the quotes, think about the questions, and practice the exercises. You WILL keep doing extraordinary things! Turn the page for your special agent Amazing Me badge!

Congratulations, you are AMAZING!

SPECIAL AGENT
AMAZING ME ACADEMY